"Coach Paye has been a gr‌   lls through-
out his career. Having personally observed his teams in action, I
have seen he's the coach to write this book. It's a must for coaches
wanting to develop their inside game."
> *Don DeVoe*
> *Head Basketball Coach*
> *U.S. Naval Academy*

"Paye presents an excellent blueprint for players or coaches to follow in developing post play on both ends of the floor. Well illustrated and basic enough for players of all ages to grasp."
> *Bill Foster*
> *Head Basketball Coach*
> *Virginia Tech*

"Coach Paye provides a comprehensive text that will be valuable to
post players and coaches at all levels. His book offers detailed information about all the important aspects of developing players who
will be effective around the basket."
> *Dave Odom*
> *Head Basketball Coach*
> *Wake Forest University*

"*Playing the Post* is an outstanding instructional guide and practice
tool. Read and use it to play better offensively and defensively in
and around the paint."
> *Kevin O'Neill*
> *Head Basketball Coach*
> *University of Tennessee*

"Coach Paye has made a science of post play. He breaks it down
into great detail with easily understood explanations and descrip-
tions."
> *Steve Robinson*
> *Head Basketball Coach*
> *University of Tulsa*

"This book has something for developing post players at all levels.
The skills that Coach Paye teaches are musts for coaches and players who are serious about the game of basketball. I'm going to use it
myself!"
> *Steve Smith*
> *Head Basketball Coach and Athletic Director*
> *Oak Hill Academy, Mouth of Wilson, VA*

PLAYING the POST

Basketball Skills and Drills

BURRALL PAYE

William Fleming High School
Roanoke, Virginia

HUMAN KINETICS

Library of Congress Cataloging-in-Publication Data

Paye, Burrall, 1938-
   Playing the post : basketball skills and drills / Burrall Paye.
     p. cm.
   Includes index.
   ISBN 0-87322-979-7
   1. Basketball--Training. I. Title
  GV885.35.P39   1996
  796.323'07--dc20   96-21956
                                            CIP

ISBN: 0-87322-979-7

Developmental Editor: Julie Rhoda; **Assistant Editor:** Sandra Merz Bott; **Editorial Assistant:** Jennifer J. Hemphill; **Copyeditor:** Bob Replinger; **Proofreader:** Jim Burns; **Graphic Artist:** Julie Overholt; **Graphic Designer:** Judy Henderson; **Photo Editor:** Boyd LaFoon; **Cover Designer:** Jack Davis; **Photographer (cover):** NBA Photos/Nathaniel Butler; **Illustrator:** Craig Ronto; **Printer:** United Graphics

Printed in the United States of America   10 9 8 7 6 5 4 3

Human Kinetics
Web site: www.humankinetics.com

United States: Human Kinetics, P.O. Box 5076, Champaign, IL 61825-5076
800-747-4457
e-mail: humank@hkusa.com

Canada: Human Kinetics, 475 Devonshire Road, Unit 100, Windsor, ON N8Y 2L5
800-465-7301 (in Canada only)
e-mail: orders@hkcanada.com

Europe: Human Kinetics, Units C2/C3 Wira Business Park, West Park Ring Road
Leeds LS16 6EB, United Kingdom
+44 (0) 113 278 1708
e-mail: hk@hkeurope.com

Australia: Human Kinetics, 57A Price Avenue, Lower Mitcham, South Australia 5062
08 8277 1555
e-mail: liahka@senet.com.au

New Zealand: Human Kinetics, P.O. Box 105-231, Auckland Central
09-523-3462
e-mail: hkp@ihug.co.nz

Contents

Drill Finder

Post-Play Drills

Key to diagrams

⑤   Player with ball

●   Ball

○   Offensive player

⑤   Numbered offensive player

X   Defensive player

X5   Numbered defensive player

〇 〇   Offensive post player's feet

▮ ▮   Defensive post player's feet

- - - - - ➤   Pass or shot

∿∿∿➤   Dribble

⟶   Cut

⋀⋁⋀➤   Shuffle

⟶▸|X5   Screen on defender

Foreword

When I was playing point guard at the University of Virginia, one of my teammates was Ralph Sampson. Ralph was one of the first players over seven-feet tall who had the talent and skills to be an offensive threat on the high post, out on a wing facing the basket, as well as in the low-post position. What 6-foot-9 Magic Johnson did to change traditional thinking about point guards, 7-foot-4 Ralph Sampson did to scrap the stereotype of post players.

Magic and Ralph had a major, lasting impact on the game. Now, the most successful teams often are comprised of interchangeable parts—players who can play any of three positions. It's not enough for shorter, quicker players to learn only perimeter skills or for taller, slower players to learn only post skills. If you're a 1, you had better be able to pop up to the high post and drive, dish, or hit the 15-footer, depending on what the defense allows.

The three-point shot, unfortunately, has fooled many players into considering a post game less important. If anything, good post skills have become *more* important with the advent of the three-point shot. On defense, a spread-out court means more one-on-one responsibility with less help from teammates. On offense, skill at passing, setting picks, and positioning is essential for post players.

As a player and coach I have witnessed the advantage held by players and teams having an effective post game over those lacking it. That's why I strongly encourage players and coaches to read and use *Playing the Post: Basketball Skills and Drills.*

Coach Burrall Paye has written an outstanding book for developing and improving high- and low-post skills. Coach Paye is an excellent teacher and clinician, combining insightful instruction with plenty of practice drills for team or individual use. His lessons on proper footwork and special tips for scoring in the post will help even the most advanced players.

Make the most of your basketball potential! Take advantage of what Coach Paye can teach you in *Playing the Post: Basketball Skills and Drills.*

Jeff Jones
Head Basketball Coach
University of Virginia

Acknowledgments

The completeness of this book is due in part to many years of listening to several people's ideas on post play. Three in particular were instrumental; two of them played for me.

Patrick, my son, contributed in a variety of ways. He has coached for two years in college and five years in high school, and is currently head coach at Northeastern High School, Elizabeth City, North Carolina. He gave me an enormous amount of knowledge on strength programs. Our many sessions at the dinner table led to trials in practice of the ideas discussed. When those trials were successful, the ideas became part of the program and now part of this book.

Barry Hamler, my longtime assistant and now head coach at Elizabeth City State University, Elizabeth City, North Carolina, played for me and showed me on the court many of the offensive moves discussed in this book. He also was one of the best offensive rebounders in the history of the state. We discussed these ideas many a night over dinner.

Andy Gray, another longtime assistant, now head coach at Garfield High School, Woodbridge, Virginia, was a great aid in the sections on shooting. Andy was a great shooter when he played and it has carried over into coaching.

Becoming a Post Player

This book is for the basketball player and coach, of either gender and at any level. Youth, middle school, high school, college, and professional players and coaches will find not only the well-known aspects of post play but golden little details never before presented in a book on basketball's post play.

What is post play? It is the play around the roughly 12-by-15-foot rectangular box on both ends of the court. This area of the court is best handled by a big person, but it does not have to be a big person. The three players listed in the acknowledgments all had excellent post-playing skills, yet one was a point guard in high school and college and one was a shooting guard-forward in high school and college. Only one was a post player.

Before most players can readily learn specific moves, they must develop physically and mentally. A physical developmental program is presented in chapter 2. Since most post players have not developed strength, the chapter offers a tried and successful weight program. Endurance, running, and coordination are usually major problems; drills are provided to correct these failings. Chapter 2 also offers quickness, agility, and jumping programs, including the quick footwork of the square drill, a drill that will geometrically improve post players' quickness.

There are five phases of development of post play—scoring, rebounding, passing, screening, and defending. Whenever a player thinks of post play, the player usually conjures up the image of a player like Hakeem Olajuwon of the Houston Rockets receiving a pass, making a move, and scoring a basket, usually on a resounding slam dunk. Chapter 3 relates the principles of scoring from the post, and chapter 4 develops scoring from the low as well as high post in eight simple, easy-to-follow steps. Techniques, strategies, and methods to improve the player in each step are offered. Drills are presented to help in this developmental process. These drills include individual drills, for players to work on while they are alone with a basketball and a goal, as well as the more familiar team-type drilling. Footwork is shown using foot drawings similar to those used to learn a dance step. Even the most inexperienced post candidate can become a dynamic scorer. The player merely needs to follow the eight steps to become proficient. If the player has difficulty mastering one of these steps—catching the ball, for example—the techniques, methods, and drills presented will help improve execution.

NBA player Dennis Rodman is an extraordinary rebounder. Chapter 5 covers the techniques, the footwork, and the little details of offensive and defensive rebounding, many of which the player or coach can see by watching Dennis Rodman play. This chapter covers savvy and drills extensively.

Chapter 6 addresses passing from every possible post angle. There is even a section on how to develop passing drills. Chapter 7 covers screening, an important fundamental in the ever-popular motion offense. Types of screens, strategies, and options are explained.

With the three-point shot becoming a major weapon in team scoring, the inside is going to be more open, more susceptible to individual play and individual attacks. The coach who does not develop a post defense, covered in chapter 8, leaves his team open for the greatest offensive onslaught in the history of basketball.

Chapter 9 gives the advanced player further skills to improve play. Players who have developed the primary two moves and the basic four moves, for example, will find a wealth of information on more advanced moves in this chapter. Coaches who need rebounding drills that go beyond the fundamentals will find in chapter 9 more complex drills to develop tireless rebounders.

How should the reader use this book? First, read all the way through it. Then begin to use the material. The reader will notice that post play is developed from many different angles. For example, pinning is covered from the offensive perspective in chapter 4 and from the defensive side in chapter 8. The reader will always have references, like "see chapter 8," when it is important to refer back or forward to certain pages. These references appear in almost all drills, making the book easier to use during those busy winter months.

After reading this book, a coach will become an expert at developing inside play. He cannot say he doesn't know how. It is here. All the little details. He cannot say he doesn't have the drills. They are here, both individual and team drills. He cannot say he doesn't have a post player. The book tells how to find, train, and develop one. Instead of just criticizing a young post player for not making a move, the coach can actually teach his young protégé how to make that move.

A prospective player cannot say she doesn't have the knowledge to develop. All the little details are in this book. Individual improvement drills are offered. Most great players are made in the summertime; the book includes an easy-to-follow, step-by-step program for off-season development. A would-be player, no matter how uncoordinated or how undeveloped, who wants to improve needs only to read this book and follow its simple step-by-step suggestions.

When you see a post player at the top of his game, how do you think he got there? Do you assume he was born there? Or do you think he learned the skills and drills of playing the post and then practiced, practiced, practiced?

Qualities of
a Post Player

Before a coach can possibly consider teaching a player how to play the post, the coach and the player must understand what is meant by the low post, the high post, and the mid post. Both must decide what they want from each post position. Both must become aware of the hard work ahead, and they must consider ways of getting that work done, from both the coach's perspective and the player's.

DEFINING THE POST POSITIONS

Diagram 1.1 shows the low-, high-, and mid-post regions. The low post is roughly rectangular in shape. One side is the baseline. Its parallel side is a line through the bottom of the broken circle parallel to the baseline. Its two perpendicular sides extend about a foot and a half outside the lane area. The big blocks, the large rectangular blocks on either side of the free throw lane, are within this space.

Any player—guard, forward, or center—can play the low-post region. Though size is often thought of as the most important requirement, drilling post-play maneuvers can benefit any player. A 6-foot-1 point guard guarded by a 5-foot-8 defender has the necessary size advantage; he has five inches on the defender. That is equivalent to a 6-foot-9 pivot player being guarded by a 6-foot-4 defender. But, in fact, the point guard might even have a

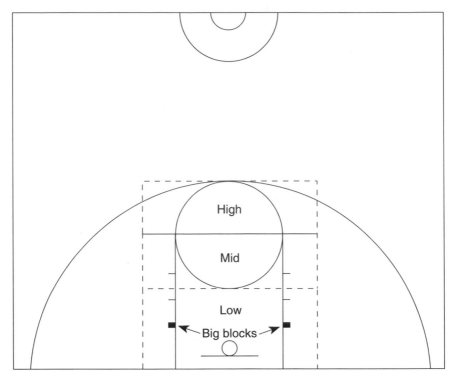

Diagram 1.1

bigger advantage as most 6-foot-4 defenders are drilled daily on low-post defense, but many 5-foot-8 defensive specialists are not.

However, with the right post-play skills, a five-inch differential between the point guard and defender is not necessarily a requirement. The attacker may be the same size as the defender, or, if exceptionally skilled, even smaller. Thus, while all tall players should immediately become low-post candidates, anyone, regardless of size, who follows the program in this book will play effectively in the post.

Now you have some idea of the floor space commonly called the low post and you have some idea of who your primary low-post candidates should be. Diagram 1.1 also displays the mid-post region. It is defined as the small rectangle from the bottom of the broken circle to the free throw line. Its perpendicular sides extend about a foot and half outside the lane.

The high-post floor position is the rectangle from the free throw line to the top of the circle. Its two perpendicular sides also extend about a foot and a half outside the free throw lane.

FIVE BASIC DUTIES OF THE THREE POST REGIONS

What do you want from your post player? Ideally, you want a scorer, a rebounder, a passer, a screener, and a defender. Fortunately, all five of these basketball skills are teachable.

Though it is best, of course, when a player has all the skills listed, excellent results can be achieved with any combination of the skills. A coach can get the maximum out of her team while players are improving their less developed skills. For example, the coach has a player with a big body and minimum foot movement skills. This big player can be effective as a screener and rebounder while foot movement is being developed. Or the coach has a tall string bean with great shooting and passing skills. The coach can put this player at the high post while developing her strength. Or the coach has a very strong, big player who does not have a shot. This player can play the low post using defense, rebounding, and screening until shooting and passing are fully developed. This is particularly what coaching at the high school level demands. It is rare that a coach receives a fully developed post player.

Versatility is best. All five basic duties of the post can be achieved with time. Have patience and work hard. The team will only be as strong as its weakest link. The coach should develop that link as she develops her team.

PLAYER CHARACTERISTICS

Different post positions are better handled by players with certain skills and physical and mental makeup. The low post is a demanding physical area, where strength is a great asset. It is best operated by a player with mental and physical toughness. Even a "wide-body" can achieve optimum results in the low post. Many muscle shots occur in the low post.

The high post, on the other hand, is best managed by a skilled passer and shooter. If this player also has driving skills, then she is a natural at the high-post position.

The mid post is a compromise between the two. It is the least drilled area of the court, both offensively and defensively. Most players play either high- or low-post positions, and most coaches teach either high- or low-post offenses. This fact alone gives the well-drilled mid-post player an unquestionable advantage. Quickness is a premium at the mid post. A player must make decisions quickly, before defensive help arrives. A shooter, a penetrator, or a power player will each find the mid post an agreeable home (fig. 1.1).

All players can learn the skills of each post position regardless of their physical and mental makeup. But a player's potential is unknown and will never be achieved until the skills of the position are fully developed. If that player aspires to be outstanding, the work to improve in these areas must be done. The work needed comes primarily from the player, but the coach also can play an important role.

Many young candidates at the post positions do not understand what is necessary to become effective post players. Gifted athletes, especially, are too often content to let their athletic ability carry them. Sadly, too many good coaches go along.

The role of the coach is to teach the elements involved in post play. The coach must exhibit enormous patience. Although the moves in this book range from the primary two through the basic four to the advanced five, few players have the footwork of the primary two, much less the basic four, when they enter college. The coach must be aware that it will take time to develop the young player and not proceed with the next step until the previous step has been mastered. Too many players will want to jump to the next step too quickly. Both player and coach must be patient.

Half-hour individual sessions before practice present a great teaching and learning time. Once players learn a skill during these sessions, they can use it forever. The book offers nine three-week training periods when the athlete can use the skills just learned.

Players are never too young to begin to learn the primary two moves. It would be ideal if the coach could get his training sessions for post players started in the lower grades in his program. The coach could use the summer months to have camps for the younger players in his area. These camps can also be useful to the varsity candidate, who can learn much by teaching the young candidate.

The coach must support his candidates by motivating them. When the going gets tough and the improvement seems slow, the youngsters, especially the ones accustomed to instant gratification (the great athlete is an example), will look for shortcuts, will look for half-steps to improvement, will even look to quit. It's the coach's job to be there to help, to motivate, and to correct fundamentals.

Coaches must not only recognize when things get slow, but also see and correct the many technical failings of their post candidates. Coaches must tell the player what is wrong and how he can correct it.Coaches organize and supervise their team's practice sessions. But

© NBA Photos/Nathaniel Butler

Figure 1.1   Hakeem Olajuwon takes a speed shot over
Shaquille O'Neal.

coaches must always remember that shooting and playing is up to
the candidate and no one else. It's now time for the coach to deputize.

The player only has one role—to be there daily, willing and able to
put forth an ample mental and physical effort. The coach does not have
to be present for the player to display this kind of commitment. The

player's role is the lonely one—just her, a basketball, a backyard goal, and a head full of dreams aiming toward reality.

ATHLETIC ABILITIES AND BASKETBALL SKILLS

What is an athlete? An athlete is an individual who is quick, who jumps well, and who runs fast. For the most part, a child is born with the muscularity that translates into quickness, speed, and vertical leap. But much can be done to improve athleticism. The next chapter offers a program that will develop strength to improve quickness, speed, and vertical leap. There is no way a 22-inch vertical leap can be turned into a 40-inch vertical leap. A player may add several inches with hard work, but no one can put in what God leaves out.

The next chapter also offers programs that improve agility, endurance, running, and coordination. Concentration and intensity are the two most important ingredients to development. Half-hearted effort elongates development. A full effort requires concentration and intensity. Both are fully developed in the drills offered throughout the book.

Shooting, dribbling, passing, screening, rebounding, fakes, and moves are the primary skills for offensive post candidates. All are learned skills; a player is not born with them. He must develop them through knowledge, repetition, and hard work.

God makes the athlete. That's his gift to the player. The player, and to some degree the coach, makes the basketball player. That's the player's gift to himself.

Post Player Developmental Program

Five physical developments must occur for the post candidate to reach her maximum potential. They are endurance, quickness and agility, jumping, running and coordination, and strength. Either the coach or the player can use this book to draw up a world-class physical developmental program—one that, in time, will be the fulfillment of youthful hopes and dreams.

Too often, a post candidate, especially a physically bigger aspirant, will give up if immediate results are not forthcoming. It is then time to mentally recall those dreams, to rededicate oneself to accomplishing those dreams, to realize again that the long haul is far more important than any short-term success or failure.

This chapter not only covers the five physical aspects but also offers many suggestions on mental attitude. It provides daily as well as off-season (spring, summer, and fall) practice programs. A young player must be willing to put forth the effort or all is lost and no improvement will occur. If the player follows the programs closely and performs with intensity, success follows naturally.

Directions for zoe
sit back relax and don't listen to this book
—Burral Paye

DEVELOPING MENTAL PREPAREDNESS

Few athletes, especially physically big players, have the proper work ethic. Most try to get along with just their athletic ability or their size. They develop few basketball skills or physical powers. Getting the big player mentally prepared and keeping him that way may be the tougher of the two tasks (mental and physical preparation). Physical preparedness can never occur unless mental preparedness continues.

Long-range goals are more important than short-range ones. The athlete must be aware of this from the beginning. If the player accepts this postulate, continuous improvement will not be a problem. Immediate success does not have to occur, for the athlete will always be looking further ahead. If the athlete does not accept this axiom, then it is best for the player to seek improvement in only one category, such as strength. Choose the category the athlete is most interested in. Learn it. Drill it. Stay with it until the athlete is encouraged about his development. After his interest is aroused and he shows some improvement, then it is time to move to the next category of physical development.

Teach to strengths and not to weaknesses if the athlete is not mentally prepared. Players like to do what they do best. It gives them a sense of accomplishment. So improve upon what the athlete does well. For example, if the athlete already has highly developed jumping and rebounding skills, develop it further by use of weights and the jumping program. After the athlete sees improvement in jumping and rebounding, it will be easier for him to see that better endurance will improve his rebounding late in a contest. Then move from endurance to quickness and agility, to running and coordination.

If the athlete is already mentally mature, he may begin by working on his weaknesses instead of his strengths. He will see the need for improvements in his weaker areas. He will even ask for help.

The mentally immature player should begin with a shorter work program. It will take him longer to develop, but any development is better than no development. Coaches should not be deceived by the tongue of the mentally immature. This player will tell you how he wants to work, to improve, to develop. But as time goes by, you will find the player offering excuses for not showing up, for begging off a difficult, often painful task. The coach must first win the athlete's heart. The coach must identify the mentally unprepared player and give him shorter workouts, teach to his strengths, and set long-range goals. Otherwise, one day the coach will find he did not have the athlete's heart, only his tongue.

Individual Improvement

Once an athlete is ready to sacrifice and is mentally mature, the player can start working on developing her skills on her own;

great improvements will follow. Use the off-season drills and programs as outlined in the chapters to follow.

Team Improvement

The coach uses drills and programs to teach his players how to, what to, and when to. How to means the actual mechanics of a skill. What to refers to deciding between two or more skills. When to relates to savvy, to knowing the actual moment to use the skill. These drills and programs are for development during the basketball season. Once the underclass students have gone through the programs during the season, they can use the ideas, techniques, and methods during the off-season for further self-improvement.

DEVELOPING THE FIVE PHYSICAL ASPECTS

Almost all taller players lack one or more of the physical prerequisites for play in the post positions. Fortunately, players can learn and develop in all five areas. It does require hard work. The book will begin outlining the strength program before moving to endurance training. It will continue with drills to improve running and coordination, jumping, and quickness and agility.

Strength Training

My strength program consists of two parts—development of the hands and weight training (figure 2.1). I have found, through years of working with post players, that poor hands are usually the greatest hindrance to success. Everything works perfectly except the post player cannot catch the pass, or fumbles the ball when rebounding it. Several ball-handling drills that improve hand strength appear in chapter 4. Below are some other suggestions.

Strengthening the Hands

- **Fingertip Push-Ups.** Have your players do as many fingertip push-ups as they can two or three times daily. Players can do these before or after practice, or while waiting to rejoin a drill. A set requires only a few seconds, but when done correctly it will improve the strength of the fingers and the wrist.

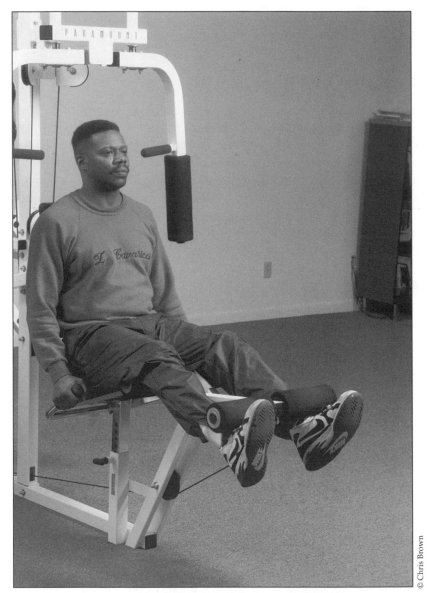

© Chris Brown

Figure 2.1   A strength program including weight training is necessary for developing post players.

- **Handgrippers or Tennis Balls.** Give athletes with unusually weak hands (fingers or wrists) a set of handgrippers. If your budget will not permit the purchase of handgrippers, tennis balls make a fine substitute. While the athlete walks from class to class, he squeezes the handgrippers or the tennis balls. Doing this six or seven times daily for a minute or two quickly develops finger and wrist strength.

- **Catching Ball off Wall.** Softness of the hands—the ability to give at the moment one receives the ball—comes with hard work. The player stands 10 feet from the wall. He throws a two-handed chest pass as hard as he can throw it and still catch it. He jumps toward this pass, landing on two feet (jump stop), and catches the ball without fumbling it. Repeat this 20 times daily. Athletes can gradually increase the hardness of the throw or decrease the distance from the wall.

- **Catching Wiffle Ball.** This drill is useful for the player who really has stone hands. The coach stands about 25 feet from the athlete and throws a regular size or softball size Wiffle ball toward the athlete, who must catch it barehanded. It does not take "stone hands" long to learn that he must give as he receives the ball or he will never catch it cleanly. This drill also develops hand-eye coordination. The player must watch the ball into his hands because it will drop, curve, or rise almost at will depending on how it is thrown (instructions come with the Wiffle ball).

Strengthening the Upper Body

Post players should use weights to develop the major muscle groups. The appropriate weight of each exercise must be determined by and for each individual. Each person must find the weight that is comfortable yet difficult. The last set of each exercise should be very difficult to perform and often unattainable. When you can do the last set without difficulty, increase the weight. It is possible to improve by adding weights to just one or more sets during a workout. For example, you could increase the weight for the last set of the bench press. This might prevent you from completing the bench press, but improvement will still occur. After completing one set, you should rest momentarily before going to the next set. Complete all bench presses, for example, before moving to the curls and so on. Also, alternate days for your weight workouts, giving each muscle group 48 hours to recover.

Many high schools, colleges, and workout centers have the machines mentioned in this section. Some centers offer discounts to students. Alternatively, you can perform a complete workout by using free weights at home. Include in your weight training a daily routine of 50 to 100 sit-ups done in sets of 20.

- **Bench Press.** Five sets of five for two weeks followed by three sets of eight for two weeks. Repeat this pattern every month; the first two weeks stress strength and the last two weeks stress muscle stamina.

Find a teammate to help. Lie flat on your back on an exercise bench with hands spaced a little more than shoulder-width apart. Start with barbell in hands and arms fully extended above the chest. Lower bar to chest and then return to full extension. Repeat until you have attempted one set of five. This develops the chest, back of upper arms, and shoulders.

- **Dumbbell Bench Press.** Five sets of five. Lying flat on back on exercise bench, place dumbbells of same weight in each hand with arms fully extended. Bring dumbbells down in bench press motion with arms a little wider than shoulder-width apart. Touch outside of chest with dumbbell and explode arms back to full extension. Repeat until you have finished one set of five. This develops the chest, triceps, and front shoulder muscles.

- **Incline Bench Press.** Three sets of five. Using dumbbells and incline bench, place dumbbells in each hand with arms extended fully from chest. Bring dumbbells down in bench press motion again with arms slightly wider than shoulder-width apart. Touch outside of chest with dumbbells and then extend arms. Repeat. This develops upper-chest and back muscles.

- **Military Press.** Four sets of five. Get a teammate to help. Begin in standing position with feet shoulder-width apart and under the bar. Hands should be gripping the bar with palms facing inward and just outside the knees. Lift barbell above the head in one continuous motion. It is at this position that you begin the military press. Lower the bar to the clavicle (in front of the head). Lift above the head until arms are fully extended. Repeat until you have attempted one set of five. This develops back of upper arms, front of shoulders, and sides of shoulders.

- **Lat Machine (if available).** Four sets of five. Using machine and lat bar, pull bar down to back of neck and slowly let bar go back to starting position. Repeat. This develops the rear shoulders, biceps, and upper-back muscles.

- **Rows.** Three sets of five. Begin in standing position. Hold barbell across thighs with arms fully extended. Palms face inward, and hands should be placed together in the middle of the bar so that the bar is balanced. While keeping the hands together, lift bar to chin by bending the elbows. Return to full extension. Repeat until you have attempted one set of five. This develops forearms, biceps, and shoulders.

✕ • **Curls.** Three sets of eight. Begin by standing with feet shoulder-width apart and arms extended, holding barbell across the thighs. Palms should be pointing outward, hands near the center of the barbell. Curl barbell upward until forearms meet biceps. Lower barbell until arms are fully extended. Repeat until you have attempted one set of eight. Be sure to keep back and legs straight. This develops the biceps.

✕ • **Dumbbell Curls.** Three sets of 16. Using dumbbells of equal weight (one in each hand), in a standing or sitting position, curl one dumbbell and, as you lower this dumbbell, begin lifting the other dumbbell. Repeat until you have done 16 curls, 8 with each arm. This develops biceps muscles.

✕ • **Twenty-ones.** One set of 21. Twenty-ones consist of three types of arm curls, each done seven times. The first type of curl is the full curl described above. On completion of the seventh full curl, the second type begins. Start at the full arm extension position and lift the barbell halfway to a full curl. On the final of the seven lifts of this half-curl, bring the bar to where the biceps and the forearms meet. This is the starting position for the third and final curl. Lower the bar to half of a full extension and bring it back to the chest. Do this seven times to complete 21 curls. Keep back and legs straight. This develops the biceps.

✕ • **Triceps Curls.** Three sets of eight. Lie flat on bench with barbell in hands, placed 8 to 12 inches apart. Start with arms fully extended. Lower bar by bending at the elbows while keeping upper arm straight. Touch bar to forehead and then extend arms. Repeat.This develops the triceps.

Strengthening the Lower Body

• **Squats.** Four sets of eight. Use a teammate helper. Place the bar on shoulder behind neck. Hands should be as wide as possible but inside the waist. Feet should be shoulder-width apart, head up, and eyes focused on a point above to keep back straight. Bend knees and hips but not the back. Lower yourself into a squatting position and then rise to a standing position. Use a bench to determine squat depth. When the rear end touches the bench and thighs are parallel to floor, rise to complete the squat. Form is most important here, and using a bench ensures proper depth. Repeat until you have completed one set of eight. This develops the thigh muscles.

*edit—notice that these exercises only need for ages 17

• **Toe-Ups.** Three sets of 20. Start in same position as squats. Use a teammate helper. Rise on toes as high as possible, remembering to keep knees locked. Lower to starting position and repeat. You can even use a board (three or four inches thick) to raise toes onto. This develops the calf muscles.

• **Step-Ups**. Three sets of eight (each leg). You will need a wooden box or platform about one to two feet tall. Standing with barbell held with both hands on back of neck or a dumbbell in each hand, step up with right foot, bring other foot up, step down with left, and step down with right. Repeat. After doing eight with one leg, switch legs. This develops thigh and hamstring muscles.

• **Lunges.** Three sets of eight. Standing with barbell on back of neck or a dumbbell in each hand, take a large step forward with one leg, and then bend the front leg and touch the back leg to the ground. Return to unbent position; then step back. Repeat eight times with each leg. This develops muscles around the knees and thighs.

• **Hamstring Curls.** Three sets of seven (if machine is available). Using hamstring curl machine, lift three sets of seven. This develops the hamstring muscles.

• **Leg Extensions.** Three sets of seven (if machine is available). Using leg extension machine, do three sets of seven. This develops the thigh muscles.

Endurance Training Drills

Basketball endurance is different from endurance in other sports. Everything in basketball occurs quickly over a short distance. Conditioning and training should emphasize short, quick bursts rather than long-distance running.

Number standards can be set for each drill. However, do not make the standards too rigid: a 6-foot-7, 280-pound post should not have the same standard as a 6-foot-7, 180-pound post. Set a standard for each post candidate. That standard should be a little out of reach. A coach needs to use good judgment to establish standards. Do not make them so modest that the player can easily obtain them.

• **Line Touching Drill.** This is the old "suicide" drill. Over the years I have found none better. The player sprints to the near foul line, back to the baseline, to the midcourt line, back to the baseline, to the far foul line, back to the baseline, to the far baseline, and back to the near baseline. The coach can alter this drill by having players jump stop at the line and then pivot, instead of just touching the line with their hands.

- **Celtics Drill.** On the first whistle, the player sprints toward the far baseline. On the next whistle, the player jump stops and begins to jump as high as he can. On the next whistle, the player begins sprinting again. When the player reaches the far baseline, bring him back with whistles. This may be repeated several times daily.

- **Pitcher's Drill.** The player is directly underneath the basket facing out of bounds. The coach is at the free throw line. The player slides from one side of the free throw lane to the other. The coach throws the ball anywhere within the lane boundaries, choosing any delivery she wishes—bounce pass, chest pass, lob, or roll. On signal (whistle or voice) the player must locate the ball, recover it, and pass it back to the coach. The player then does a 180-degree turn, landing in a jump stop and facing out of bounds. The drill continues. Use this drill for up to one and one-half minutes. This drill not only improves endurance but also helps improve the post candidate's hands.

- **Lane Touching Drill.** The player is in defensive position, facing midcourt. The player slides from one side of the lane to the other, touching outside the lane without bobbing the head. Begin this drill with a duration of half a minute and work up to a minute and a half.

- **Monkey Drill.** The player begins at one corner of the court. He gets in a defensive position, touching the palms of his hands on the court. He slides the length of the baseline, touching his palms on the floor after every slide. He must not cross his feet. He now slides up the sideline until he reaches midcourt. He slides across the midcourt line. He goes down the sideline to the far baseline, slides the far baseline, and comes up the sideline to midcourt. He slides the midcourt line to the near sideline and slides the near sideline to the corner where he started. After every slide he touches his palms on the floor. Because this is such a demanding drill, do not use it before or during practice; it takes too much out of the player. As an after-practice drill, it can develop great endurance.

Running and Coordination Drills

Training programs are not isolated—they overlap. For example, the pitcher's drill above develops endurance and develops the hands. There is some running in the endurance program, and there is some endurance in any proper weight program. It is up to the coach to decide which part of which program is best suited for a particular athlete.

- **Running the Lines Drill.** Players use the perimeter boundary lines. As they run the coach will shout instructions and footwork commands. Commands are push left-go right, push right-go left, skip, dribble-slide (see chapter 3), drop step, turn backward, etc. Once the player executes the command, he begins running again, waiting for the next command.
- **Backward Wave Drill.** Players line up in a defensive stance. The coach stands on the baseline with players in front of him. Players watch the coach. The coach signals the players which way to slide defensively by waving his hands. Sprinting forward and backward can also be incorporated into this drill.
- **Big Man's Fast-Break Drill (drill 4).** This drill is presented in chapter 4 because it involves pure basketball training as opposed to just physical training.
- **Run Full Court Well Drill (drill 5).** See chapter 4.

Jumping

While jumping is an athletic ability given at birth, a player can improve slightly with proper drilling, especially in the second and third effort (some say this is more endurance training than jumping).

- **Rim Touching Drill.** Jump up and touch the rim (bottom of board or bottom of net) 10 times with the right hand, 10 times with the left hand, 10 times with left hand and right hand as a double touch, and finally 10 times with both hands simultaneously.
- **Jumping With Weights Drill.** Put a spot on the floor with tape. Players must land in this spot every time. Put on lead weights (chest jacket, weighted shoes, etc.). If you do not have a weighted jacket, you can create a substitute by putting a belt through free weights and tying tightly to the body. Alternatively, jump in galoshes. Do the rim-touching drill above.
- **Straddle Jumps Drill.** Player jumps up, bringing his feet up toward his chest where he touches the feet with the hands. Do this 20 times without stopping.
- **Rope Jumping Drill.** Do exercises with both feet and then with one foot. Then use alternating feet. Start with normal jumping. Advance to arms crossing and other more difficult stunts with the ropes.

Quickness and Agility

As stated before, these programs are not isolated. Rope jumping, for example, improves jumping and agility. The better the coach recognizes what her athlete needs, the better she can prescribe the cure (see next section).

• **Footwork Square Drill.** Make a letter X with tape or paint on the floor. Make each part about 3 feet apart (diagram 2.1). Begin drill with one foot on each end part, like D and E. Jump into the middle, C in diagram 2.1, with both feet, then out to A and B. Pivot while jumping slightly. Your left foot was on A. After the pivot, it will be on B. Return both feet to C; then jump back out to D and E.

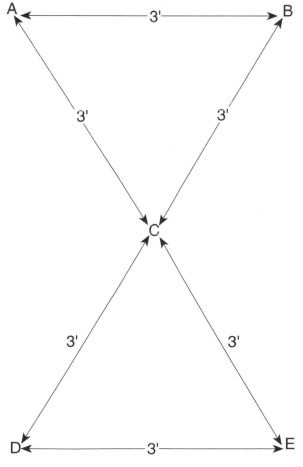

Diagram 2.1

Your right foot should be on D and your left foot on E. Pivot by jumping slightly. Your left foot is now on D and your right foot on E. Continue this drill for 30 seconds, counting and recording each full revolution.

Now you are ready to begin a second phase of the drill. You jump into the middle, the C in diagram 2.1, with only your right foot. Jump out with both feet, right foot landing on B and left stopping on A. Pivot by jumping slightly, letting right foot go to A and left to B. Continue this part of the drill for 30 seconds, counting and recording each full revolution.

Now go to the third phase of the drill. You jump into the C, the middle, with only the left foot. Jump out with left foot landing on A and right on B. Pivot by jumping slightly, letting right foot land on A and left on B. Continue this for 30 seconds, counting and recording each full revolution.

Now begin the fourth phase. You start with your back to the X. That is, you start with your right foot on D and left foot on E. Jump backward into C landing on both feet. Then jump out with right foot on A and left foot on B. Pivot by jumping slightly. Now your left foot is on A and your right foot is on B. Jump into the middle, C, landing on both feet. Jump out to D and E. Pivot and continue the drill for 30 seconds. Count and record each full revolution.

If you keep an accurate chart, you will notice you are completing more revolutions with each day. You will begin to barely move off the floor with each jump. Your toes will begin to grab at the floor. This is real quickness. You can increase the timing of each portion of the drill up to one and one-half minutes. This also serves as a great endurance drill.

• **Carioca.** Players stand at midcourt, planning to move from sideline to sideline. The coach stands out front. Players keep their hips parallel to the coach. Players begin footwork motion by placing left foot in front of right, step with right, place left foot behind right, step with right, and so on, continuing to the sideline. Players then do the opposite as they carioca back to the other sideline. Begin this as a 30-second drill and work up to one minute.

• **Ballhandling Drills.** Post candidates should perform the guard's ballhandling drills, especially the ones requiring movement. This greatly improves running, coordination, agility, and endurance. Take one ball and dribble the length of floor doing the crossover, then the spin, and then the half-spin (this also helps in post moves; see chapter 3). Do this right-handed and left-handed, down and back before changing starting hand. Now take two balls and repeat the crossover, spin, and half-spin by using alternating heights of dribble and then same heights of dribble. This gives each player 12 trips up and down the floor—right-handed with all three, left-handed with all three, alternating heights with all three, and same heights with all three. Each ballhandling scheme not only improves the move (see chapter 4) but also develops excellent coordination and feel for the ball (do not let players look at the ball).

To perform the crossover, the player places his left foot ahead and in front of his body while dribbling to his right. At the moment of the crossover, the player drops his left foot and crosses the ball over to his left hand, establishing the right foot as the front foot and the left hand as the dribbling hand. When two balls are used in the drill above, only the footwork is done, but the two balls must be controlled while doing the footwork.

When executing the spin dribble, the dribbler will have his left foot forward while dribbling to his right. At the moment of the spin, the dribbler plants the left foot as a pivot foot and pulls the ball with the right hand as he makes the full 360-degree pivot. He then switches the ball to the left hand while the right foot is now forward and the body protects the ball. When two balls are used, only the footwork is done but both balls must be controlled.

The half-spin is accomplished by dribbling to the right with the left foot forward, beginning the spin move by pivoting on the left foot and pulling the ball with the right hand. But this pivot is only 90 to 180 degrees. The dribbler then spins back in the same direction as he began by pushing off the right foot and picking up the left foot. When two balls are used, only the footwork is drilled but both balls must be controlled.

The coach may want to incorporate these ballhandling drills:

- Move ball in circular motion around the body standing and running.
- Move ball around both legs standing and running.
- Tip ball on fingertips standing and running.
- Dribble ball between the legs standing and running.
- While in a squatting position with both hands on ball in front of body, drop ball between legs and catch it with both hands behind body.
- With one hand in front of body and one hand behind, drop ball and switch hands, catching the ball before it hits ground.

DOING THE ACTUAL WORK

Few players enjoy the hard developmental work. They would rather play, and, frankly, I don't blame them. They are young and do not understand, for the most part, how important it is to develop physically and mentally. Many recognize the importance of improving their basketball skills, but few respond positively to physical developmental work. The coach must know and motivate his players.

Daily Practice Work

Because the post area is so vital, as a coach I frequently use the first half hour before "regular" practice to develop basketball skills. Each player picks up his work schedule and a ball. This daily work schedule will not change until the player shows considerable progress. Each player begins his own drills. It serves as a good warm-up to practice. If practice is from 3:30 to 5:00, I expect the player to be at his work station by 3:00.

The player will work hard at this time since the coaches observe and correct. I limit each athlete to two or three programs that I consider vital to his improvement. A typical daily practice routine includes 30 minutes on individual work, an hour and a half on team drills, and 20 minutes of weights after practice.

If a player is having trouble catching the ball, I would include many of the catching drills. If he is having trouble getting position, I would have the athlete work on positioning. If he is not smooth with his moves, I demand the moves drills. If the player has trouble in more than one area, which most do, I divide the 30 minutes into improvement segments but never emphasize more than two areas of improvement at any one practice session.

Let's say Player A has stone hands. Nothing can be accomplished until those hands improve. His program will include the following:

Fingertip push-ups	3 minutes
Catching Wiffle ball	5 minutes
Ballhandling	6 minutes
Catching ball off wall	3 minutes
Pitcher's drill	3 minutes
Big man's fast-break drill	10 minutes

Let's say Player B is not exceptionally quick, lacks endurance, and needs work on his moves. His program will include the following:

Footwork square drill	4 minutes
Toss ball out and make move drill (DeVoe drill)	6 minutes
Big man's fast-break drill	10 minutes
Rebounding drills	10 minutes

Players A and B could work together at a single basket if space or staffing is a problem, but Player A would do his 30-minute program while Player B is working on his 30-minute program. Use managers as helpers.

All post players work on their weight programs after practice. I abbreviate lifting to about 20 minutes during the season. The other coaches and I evaluate which part of each player's muscularity needs the most work and assign the appropriate exercises.

Off-Season Plans

This is the most important part of the year for development. It is the time when the greats and the near greats improve the most.

Of course, if you have a mentally immature candidate, you would not want to overload him. He would not do the work, and you would be hurting his future development by allowing him to take shortcuts. Just give him a few things to do, and daily encourage and direct him on those.

Each player has a different off-season program. The player follows the program for three weeks before it is upgraded or changed. There are nine three-week programs; all contain weights and fundamentals. The remainder of the program varies with the individual.

A typical beginning three-week program for a motivated, mentally mature post candidate follows.

Monday through Saturday

Weight program
- Upper body—Monday, Wednesday, and Friday.
- Lower body—Tuesday, Thursday, and Saturday.

Monday through Friday

Fundamentals

- Blasting-out drill (drill 18; see chapter 5).
- Power Pick-Up Drill, a variation of Mikan shooting drill (drill 7; see chapter 4).
- Toss ball out and make move drill (the DeVoe drill; see chapter 4).
- Ballhandling drills (chapter 2).
- Free throws (make seven in a row after each drill).

Tuesday and Thursday

Endurance

- Line touching 5 minutes.
- Lane touching 3 minutes.

Jumping

- Rim touching 5 minutes.

Catching

- Toss ball off wall drill 3 minutes.

Agility and Coordination

- Jump rope 10 minutes.

Players work with upper-body weights on Monday, Wednesday, and Friday and with lower-body weights on Tuesday, Thursday, and Saturday. I ask players to work on fundamentals daily and on the other parts on Tuesday and Thursday. Athletes are to play on Monday, Wednesday, and Friday, using newly trained skills. After finishing their programs, which usually require less than an hour per day, I encourage the players to play half court three-on-three or full court five-on-five. During those games, the candidates should use the new fundamentals or moves they are learning—spin moves or busting out on rebounds, for example.

The following is a fun one-on-one drill for players to work on their new skills. Player A passes to Player B with Player C defending. If Player B scores, she gets 1 point, and Player B stays on offense. Player A becomes the new defender while Player C becomes the passer. If Player B does not score, Player C can rebound and score. Player C gets the point while Player A becomes the new defender and Player B the new passer. The game goes to 11 points.

As the post candidate nears the end of the ninth program, she should show remarkable progress. The coach should add to the fundamentals as the weeks pass. For example, the earlier three-week program might only include drop steps and turnarounds (see chapter 4) for moves and shots. But when the 27th week is over, the post candidates should be adept at crossover drives, spins, and half-spins as well as shots off each of those moves.

SKILLS WRAP-UP

Development of the body, mentally as well as physically, is the subject of chapter 2. Improvement occurs faster when the athlete is stronger, quicker, more agile, and has greater endurance. The teaching and learning of the skills in the chapters that follow can occur simultaneously with the building of the body discussed here.

Continue strength training, endurance programs, running and coordination drills, jumping programs, and quickness and agility drills even as the athlete begins to develop his basketball skills. Chapter 3 begins the development of those basketball skills with the basic slide step, the slide-step dribble, and the jump stop—each fundamental to post play.

3

Ten Principles of Scoring in the Post

A coach should not limit her post-up play to a tall pivot player. Anyone who has size and possesses post knowledge and skills may post up. A quickness advantage, regardless of size, often leads to scoring from a post-up position.

Size and quickness cannot be taught; but skills and knowledge can. The legendary Walter "Buck" Van Huss at Kingsport Dobyns-Bennett High School, Kingsport, Tennessee, posted his point guard in a year when he had an exceptional 6-foot-5 point guard. Coach Denny Crum at the University of Louisville loves to post his big guards. It is a part of his offensive system. I always posted my scoring forward as part of the offensive system. Almost all coaches have plans allowing them to post their power forwards. Any player, male or female, regardless of starting floor position, can score from the post positions by learning the skills and knowledge of posting.

Two primary examples of players who have worked hard to develop low-post technique and savvy are David Robinson and Charles Barkley. One is a tall, lanky 7-footer while the other is a stout, hardy 6-foot-4. Both play at the highest level, the National Basketball Association. Both are stars. Both have great natural outside games—Barkley on the perimeter and Robinson at the high post (see figure 3.1). Both have fully developed, superb low-post techniques.

Who could have foretold, for example, that David Robinson, who then was only 6-foot-5, had such low-post potential when he played at Osbourn Park High School before enrolling at Navy? Certainly not me, even though I had scouted Osbourn Park several times since they are in our region. Work ethic, desire for knowledge, and the will to be the very best are ingredients that are hard to scout. It's hard to see what is inside the player; it's hard to tell a book by its cover.

Any player with the same work ethic, the same desire for knowledge, the same willpower needs only to follow the outlines in this book to obtain the necessary skills, strength, and knowledge. If God has granted superb athleticism and size to that player, stardom is only a few years of practice away.

Regardless of whom the coach decides to post up—a guard, a forward, or a center—the coach will want them to follow these ten

Figure 3.1   David Robinson executes a jump shot.

guiding rules while playing the post. By adhering to these ten axioms, players will have fewer turnovers, they will play under more control, they will play smarter, and they will score more often and with better shots. These are the basics of post play.

OPPORTUNITY

Post players seize the opportunities given by their defenders. They do not force the play. The post attacker takes advantage of the defender's mistakes, sometimes even luring the defender into making a mistake. After the defender makes a mistake, the post player, by following the principles here, will not allow the defender to recover. A post player will let the defender set up the option he will use. He even lets the defender dictate the shot. The attacker at the low post is already in the highest percentage shooting area; there are no bad shots here. So it does not matter which shot he takes. They are all good. The principle here is this: Seize the opportunity; do not force the play.

PLAY OFF BOTH FEET

Low-post attackers must make use of two pivot feet. This gives them greater deception in their moves. Because they have two pivot feet, defenders must guess from which direction the attack will come.

By having both feet on the floor the attacker has better balance from which to launch the move, better balance for the shot, and better balance and strength for holding body position. Movement off two feet is much quicker than movement off one foot. The only movement possible off one foot is in the direction opposite that foot or a complete front or reverse pivot. A good defender knows this and plays the quick move away from the one foot before playing a pivot (reverse or front). A defender figures she has time to recover on the slower reverse or front pivots. Playing off two feet means quickness in either direction and leaves the defender guessing, a decided advantage for the attacker.

Two feet also give the attacker greater strength and more explosive power, especially on her jumps. It would be difficult to imagine stopping, stepping, and shooting a power layup without first gathering both feet underneath the body before exploding into the air. This gathering of two feet underneath the body gives balance for the shot and strength for the possible three-point play off the power layup. Unless the attacker uses both feet the defender can easily knock the shooter off balance and eliminate the easy power layup.

Proper use of two feet gives better balance, more deception, greater strength, and quicker movement. One foot gives the defender the advantage. *So play off both feet.*

Playing off two feet makes the jump stop much more important than the stride stop. The players can practice the jump stop in many of the drills and developmental programs. For example, while running the Celtics drill (see chapter 2), the post players stop in a jump stop before they begin jumping. Many of the endurance drills in chapter 2 feature the jump stop. The coach should observe the jump stop first before any move to be sure the jump stop is mechanically correct. To jump stop (drill 1), the attacker lands on both feet simultaneously, creating two pivot feet. The player lands on the heel, switching the weight forward to the balls of the feet. At the same moment, the player lowers the center of gravity by bending at the knees and waist, almost in a squat or sitting position. The degree of the squat depends on the speed at the moment of the jump stop. The greater the speed, the more pronounced the squat. The feet should end slightly wider than the shoulders.

[handwritten margin note: Jump stop land on heels and switch weight forward]

USE SLIDE STEPS

Movement of the feet in the post is extremely important. The low-post attacker always wants to keep his feet under him so he can use both feet at all times. Slide steps enable him to do this.

The slide step also allows the low-post player to keep his dribble between his legs. This helps protect the ball from a perimeter player who sags off to help low-post defenders. The body of the low-post attacker protects the slide-step dribble from the low-post defender (see figure 3.2).

The slide step permits the low post to keep both feet under him, giving better balance, more strength, and quicker movements. It also guarantees two pivot feet, permitting quicker pivots when the low post considers his offensive move. To teach the slide step, refer to drill 2.

Figure 3.2   Charles Barkley uses a slide-step dribble.

STRENGTH

Low-post scorers must be stronger than their defenders if they are to operate at maximum efficiency. The low-post area is the three-point scoring area. Strength permits the attacker to maintain balance and control on his shots while being fouled around the basket.

Chapter 2 presented a strength program designed to improve all the body parts necessary to score at the low post. The low-post candidate who closely follows that program will strengthen the muscles most needed to play the low post. Strength will also improve coordination, quickness, and mobility. There are other things that a low-post player can do to strengthen herself around the basket. She can

- play on both feet;
- throw her head back and tense up her back muscles to make herself stronger for shooting power shots;
- stiffen her forearms to provide strength for posting up the defender and holding the ball; and
- grip the ball tighter, using fingertips and not the palms, to make it harder for a defender to jar the ball loose on a shot or before a shot.

Players who improve their strength improve their scoring potential. Strength is a major principle in scoring from the low post.

EXPOSURE OF THE BALL

Keep ball exposure to a minimum. The longer the ball is exposed, the greater the opportunity for a steal or a blocked shot.

In teaching all aspects of low-post scoring, a coach must consider how long she wants the ball exposed. In the scheme presented in this book, you will notice players offer the ball to the defense in only two maneuvers, a dribble and a fake. First, the dribble: I teach the slide-step dribble, trying to protect the dribble as best we can from the perimeter defenders with our legs and from the post defender with our bodies. Proper drilling (see drill 2) eliminates most of these errors. Second, the fake: I teach a pump fake that improves a player's opportunity to get off a good shot, frequently resulting in a three-point play. Proper execution of the pump fake (see chapter 4 for mechanics and drill) reduces ball exposure and eliminates any blocked shots. Proper drilling and proper execution reduce steals and blocked shots due to limited exposure of the ball.

There is one other time when the low-post player exposes the ball momentarily. It occurs only when the low-post player uses a basic move (see chapter 4, "The Move"). The low-post attacker will momentarily show the ball to the defender playing behind her before she pivots in the opposite direction or drop steps on the side of the exposure. She does this to put pressure on the basket when a defender tries to play behind her. Such defenses usually occur when the attacking player is quicker than her defender. This low-post move (see chapter 4, "The Move") gets her defender in motion and often results in a drive to the basket and a three-point play.

LEVERAGE

This is the most vital principle of low-post play. The attacker must control the defender. To do this, the low-post defender uses proper foot and body movement and contact (see this chapter, "Body Positioning" and chapter 4, "Positioning"). Yes, contact. The attacker maintains positioning on the defender by keeping body contact with the defender. The low post keeps this contact by feeling the defender with his rear, his arms, and his hands. This is called pinning; the principle is leverage.

The low-post attacker must maintain leverage. Once the attacker gains positioning, he never lets go. He keeps it. (How he keeps it is explained in detail in this chapter, "Body Positioning.") The defender must back off and lose contact before he can regain defensive positioning. This is called avoiding the pin (see chapter 8). Coaches should teach avoiding the pin early so their defenders will be better defenders than anyone the attackers face all year. This means your practices in posting and avoiding the pin will be equivalent to or better than any performed during games. Every team and individual drill will involve pinning and avoiding the pin. Your drills, of course, will emphasize other things, but these drills must always include posting and post defense as long as you are working on shooting and scoring. The low-post attacker will be trying to maintain leverage at all times; the defender will be trying to avoid the leverage (see figure 3.3).

CONTROL YOUR DEFENDER

Control of the defender begins before leverage is used. The low-post attacker encourages the defender to make a mistake; then the

Figure 3.3 After getting into a post-up position on the big block, David Robinson uses leverage to hold his position.

attacker does not let the defender recover (leverage). He gains this control by varying his position on the court and on his defender. He prevents and inhibits his defender's movement by using the tactics described in the section on positioning. He begins this control by racing to the big block on the first possession of the game. The attacker studies the position of his defender, makes his adjustments, and begins his control. When the defender attempts to change his position, the attacker counters him with exactly the correct move at exactly the right time.

Teamwork also helps the low-post player control his defender. By knowing his team's offensive attack, the low post can anticipate the next perimeter pass before the defender does and put his defender at a disadvantage (see chapter 4).

A third method of control involves the revolutionary roll maneuver. This technique, when done correctly, cannot be defended (see drill 3; chapter 4). This maneuver regains control by the offense even when the defense has established perfect defensive position.

Control of your defender comes when you understand completely how to play the low post. Savvy is the knowledge of fundamentals, the art of always being in the right place, the "feel" for the game demonstrated by one's performance. Controlling a defender is a one-on-one mental chess game, played at top speed and quickness, using moves, strength, and leverage.

EXPECT HELP DEFENDERS

Whenever passes come into the low post, there are a myriad of defensive techniques to force the ball back out. Rarely does the low post have the luxury of one-on-one combat unless he moves quickly. Help comes from a variety of sources—double-down from strong side, double-down from weak side, and rotation from weak side are the major three. The section on savvy in chapter 4 covers these and other defensive techniques. Concentration by the attacker and constant drilling on the savvy drills allows the low post to learn when to make each maneuver. The important principle here is to always expect help defenders whenever you receive the ball at the low post. The low-post attacker's moves must be quick and her judgment sound. Both are learnable aspects of low-post play.

SHOOTING POSITION

All low-post players can become proficient at shooting near the basket. I teach only three shots—the turnaround bank shot, the hook layin, and the muscle shot. All three are nearly 100 percent shots. My assistants and I even took a 6-foot-6, 240-pound defensive tackle off the football team and taught him to score from these three shots (he later played football for the University of Virginia, the New York Jets, the Miami Dolphins, and the Kansas City Chiefs). He became a very proficient shooter. The bank shot hits the same spot on the board over and over. This is easy for any semicoordinated person. The other two shots are layups.

Because of the contact that occurs near the basket, the low-post attacker wants to bank the ball higher off the board. This allows the attacker to score even when being fouled, gaining a three-point attempt.

A low-post attacker must have both arms free when he shoots. The low post must shoot off both legs. He must be patient and take the time to square up to the basket. He never wants to aim his shoulders at the basket. All the attacker's moves, when executed properly, place him in proper shooting position.

BODY POSITIONING

All scoring begins from proper body positioning, which refers not only to position on the defender but also to the attacker's position on the court. When you make your first trip to the big block, you must see how your defender intends to play you. On the next trip down the court you adjust your position on the floor to take maximum advantage of the defensive position, opening up a bigger scoring area (see chapter 4, "Positioning").

After you get proper floor position, you want to get proper post-up position on your defender. When you get post-up position, use leverage to maintain it. Position on the floor and position on your defender make up the two parts of proper body positioning.

SKILLS WRAP-UP

The cardinal rules of post play are presented in ten easy-to-follow principles. They can be combined into two basic ideas—getting proper position on the floor and getting proper position on the defender. When the post player is out of position, he can regain it by correct use of the ten principles. These ten rudiments show how a post player can coax the defender into mistakes; then the post player prevents the defender from ever recovering.

Without the basic beginnings of movement—the jump stop, slide step, and slide-step dribble—as a foundation, future learning of basketball skills is difficult if not impossible. The jump stop starts positioning and the slide step and the slide-step dribble begin the move. The eight steps that follow in chapter 4 will see the player through the reception of the pass and the completion of the move.

1 Jump Stop Drill

Objectives

1. To learn the jump stop (can vary speed).
2. To mentally anticipate scoring moves (see chapter 9, "Post Scoring Theory").
3. To physically feel both feet as pivot feet.

Procedure

1. Line up all post candidates under the basket (see diagram).
2. Player 1 breaks toward the coach and jump stops.
3. The coach passes the ball directly to Player 1 or on one side or the other.
4. The post player checks left and right, firmly feeling both feet on the ground. The post player thinks about her move while she is checking directions (see chapter 9, "Post Scoring Theory").
5. Post Player 1 passes the ball back to the coach, breaks to the opposite side of the court, jump stops, and receives a pass from a second coach. The post player checks direction again, considering her move mentally while feeling both feet on the ground.
6. Post Player 2 breaks to the first coach when post Player 1 breaks to the second coach.

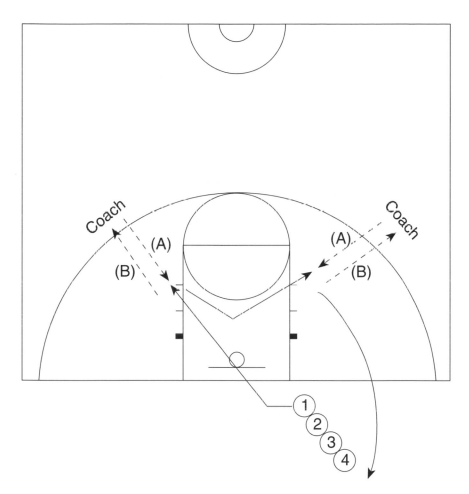

Drill 1   Jump stop drill.

2 Slide-Step Dribble Drill

Objectives

1. To learn the slide-step dribble, a dribble used in drop-step moves, spin moves, half-spin moves, as well as other moves and maneuvers of chapters 4 and 9.
2. To correct incorrect foot movement.
3. To learn that the slide-step dribble allows the post to move with the basketball without walking and without sacrificing proper foot movement. In the low-post area, proper foot movement is extremely important.

Procedure

1. Line up low-post candidates at the baseline side of the free throw lane.
2. The first player steps out with a basketball. He slides around the low-post area (see chapter 1) and then returns. He takes only one dribble, catches the ball, and establishes a low crouched position with two pivot feet. Then he dribbles again, catches the ball, and establishes the low crouched position. He does it again until he has gone to the opposite big block. After his first slide-step dribble, the second player in the line begins. When the first player reaches the opposite big block, he waits until the others join him. When all have reached the opposite big block, they return. The coach can require players to do this once or several times. The coach must be satisfied with the slide-step dribble because it is so important for effective low-post play.
3. To slide-step dribble, the low post begins by moving his front foot in the direction he is going. This is a long step. Say he begins with the right foot. He dribbles once with his opposite hand, the left hand in this case. The dribble is directly between his legs. This prevents perimeter defenders from slapping the dribble away. They will slap the legs of the low-post dribbler. The dribble must be a low, quick dribble. The dribble is followed by a long, quick left-foot step. The attacker puts both hands on the dribble as the left foot hits the floor. This permits the player to use either foot as a pivot foot (if going in the

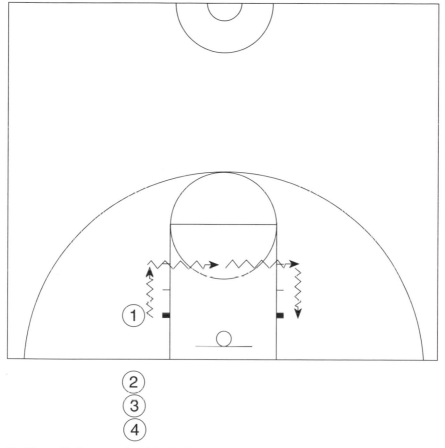

Drill 2   Slide-step dribble drill.

other direction, lead with the left foot, followed by a dribble, followed by the right foot). The player brings ball quickly and strongly in tight to his body. This reduces exposure.

4. After the low post has mastered a one-dribble slide step, the coach can move to a two-dribble slide step. Under no circumstance should the coach teach a three-dribble slide step. Three dribbles would result in a three-second call as well as all kinds of defensive perimeter help.

Becoming a Scorer in the Post

A player must correctly perform eight steps to score from the post positions. He must get open, receive a pass, make a move, and score. If the player blunders on any of the eight steps, he will not score. By dividing scoring into eight steps, the player can easily see which require more work and which do not. Using the drills and foot diagrams will guide players through the movements until they become second nature.

EIGHT STEPS TO SCORING

Scoring from the low post involves eight steps.

1. **Getting Open**: The player must get open. Post players can do this with proper cutting mechanics.
2. **Positioning**: Alternatively, the attacker can get open by getting proper positioning.
3. **The Target**: To make things easier for the perimeter passer to get the ball to the post player, the post player provides a target.
4. **The Pass**: The fourth step is the actual pass. This is a coordinated effort between the passer and the post player.
5. **The Catch**: The post player must make the catch. Post players must develop their hands so that they catch the pass firmly yet softly. Post players fumble many passes.

6. **The Move**: After cleanly receiving the pass, the post player can begin the move.
7. **The Shot**: The post player then decides on the shot.
8. **The Savvy—Knowing When**: The eighth step comes in knowing when, not just what and how. This is called savvy.

Problems and errors can develop in any of the eight steps. Each step will be presented separately with drills and programs to help correct any failings. Advanced moves will be presented for those star players who master the fundamentals and need to move on. If a player is having trouble scoring from the post, the attacker needs only check which of the eight steps is preventing the score from developing. Restudying that step and relearning its mechanics and strategies will get the post player scoring efficiently.

Getting Open

There are many team maneuvers a coach can use to get his player open at the low post. But the purpose of this book is not to choose team offensive methods; it is to develop the post individually. With this in mind, five strategies will be presented for getting open—three when breaking from the weak side and two while on the strong side. The ball side is called the strong side, and the side opposite the ball is the weak side.

From the weak side the low-post player determines if the ball is above the low-post area (see diagram 1.1), if the ball is low near the baseline, or if the ball is going to be reversed. The location of the ball determines which of the three moves the low post will use.

When the ball is high, the low-post player on the weak side breaks directly along the line connecting the big blocks. Regardless of where the ball is, the cutting low post will reach a point near the basket area where her defender is at a disadvantage. The defender gets to a point where it is hard to see both the ball and her assigned player. Usually the defender is taught to block the cutter's path toward the ball. When the cutter sees the body check about to occur, she makes a long step with the foot nearest the midcourt line. This must be an exaggerated long step. Then, in a crossover step, the low-post player swings her other foot between the defender and the ball (see figure 4.1). The attacker wants to make contact with her defender. After doing this, the low-post cutter moves out of the lane using slide steps, tries to hold her position, and gives the target for a pass with the hand nearest midcourt. The defender must recover to the high

Figure 4.1   David Robinson pivots into a face-up position before beginning his move.

side, or a pass inside followed by the drop step inside gives the low-post attacker a layup. Should the defender recover to the high side, the roll (see drill 3) restores proper offensive positioning.

When the ball is low, near the baseline, the low-post, weak-side player breaks across the height of the low-post area (see diagram 1.1). She breaks to a spot that is not advantageous to the defender. At this moment, the low-post cutter takes an exaggerated long step with the baseline foot. She swings her midcourt foot through between herself and her defender (crossover step). She makes contact and tries to hold it, sliding out of the lane using slide steps. She should be above the big block. She uses her baseline hand as a target hand. The defender must recover low side or at least front the attacker. If she doesn't, the low-post player can receive a pass, drop step, and shoot the power layup. If the defender recovers, the roll recovers proper position for the attacker.

In either of the last two maneuvers the low-post attacker does not want to fight the defensive recovery. In fact, the attacker might even encourage the defender to recover because the roll then becomes unstoppable. If the defense does not stop the initial cut, the low-post attacker receives the pass and makes an easy shot. If the defender stops the initial cut, she leaves herself vulnerable to the roll. Either way, the offense wins.

The third weak-side cut is called weak-side pinning. This occurs when the weak-side defender, X5 in diagram 4.1, has established proper weak-side defensive positioning and the low-post attacker knows the ball is going to be reversed. 5, in diagram 4.1, shows 1, who has the ball, the back of her hand. This signals 1 that 5 wants the ball reversed to 2. While the ball is being reversed, 5 has stepped two steps or so toward X5. 5 keeps the legs spread shoulder-width or farther apart. When the ball is reversed, X5 will try to get around 5 to establish a new strong-side defensive position. When X5 takes the first defensive step, 5 slides one step with X5. On X5's next step, 5 reverse pivots. This simple maneuver puts X5 on 5's back. 5 uses leverage to maintain this positioning. A pass inside gives 5 a golden opportunity for a drop-step layup. This maneuver was expertly used by the great UCLA teams under Coach John Wooden.

Fronting and the unstoppable roll make up the two strong-side maneuvers. Fronting is when the defender plays in front of the low-post attacker. This is covered in "Positioning."

The roll is used to regain proper position from an excellent defender. Drill 3 shows the first part of strong-side drilling. 5 could have begun on the strong side or he could have cut to the strong

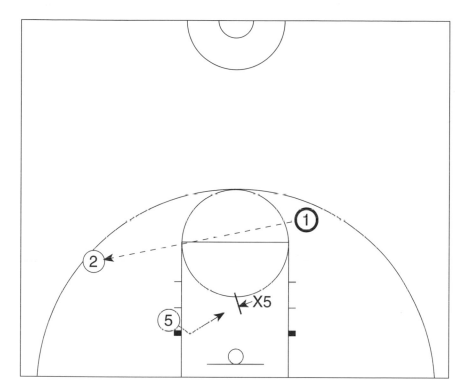

Diagram 4.1

side, using one of the cuts described above. If 1 has the ball, X5 must be on the top side of 5, fronting (or three-quartering) him. If X5 is below 5, 1 could easily pass inside to 5 for the drop-step hook layin (see drill 3). 5 tries to get his front foot (right foot) in front of X5's front foot (see "Positioning"). If X5 has established good position, 5 does not fight the positioning farther than one step from the lane. As 1 passes to 3, 5 allows X5 to go over the top. If X5 decides to go behind 5, 5 pins him, gets the pass, makes the move, and scores. So X5 must go over the top. As X5 assumes proper low-side fronting (or three-quartering) positioning, 5 reverse pivots, using his right foot as his pivot foot. Now 5 has at least a half-body advantage on X5. A pass back out to 1 makes the pass inside extremely easy. This move, called the roll, will always give 5 the post-up position. It is really the only strong-side maneuver a player needs to learn, but the buttonhook will be presented for a corner or wing player cutting from strong-side corner or wing to strong-side low post.

The buttonhook is the other strong-side cutting maneuver. Knowledge of how the defender intends to play strong-side post defense aids the buttonhook maneuver. Most coaches have a well-defined theory on defending the big block and they teach their defense based on it. One scouting report would reveal the defensive scheme.

A player, during a game, can derive the same knowledge in a possession or two. The key is knowing where the defender fronts the low post. Certainly it would not occur too far from the lane. To front a few feet outside the lane opens the area near the basket for a lob pass and a power layup.

Armed with that knowledge, the buttonhook player jump stops just short of the projected defensive fronting. The attacker is facing the defender while approaching the post area. The attacker simply reverse pivots into the defender to gain position before the defender can establish a three-quartering or full-fronting position. The attacker chooses to reverse pivot on the high side if the defender is higher than the attacker and on the low side if the defender is lower than the attacker. (The attacker usually knows the defensive philosophy, which dictates the defender's position.) This reverse pivot gains proper positioning on the floor and on the defender for the pass and the move.

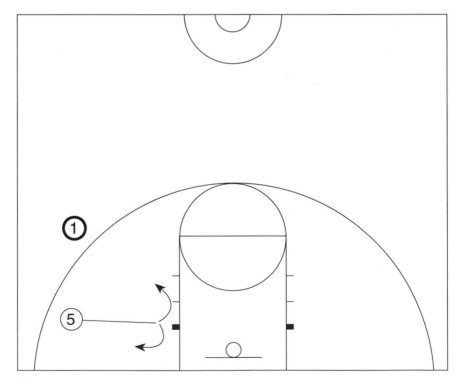

Diagram 4.2

If the defender has played low side, 1 simply passes to 5 for the drop-step hook (diagram 4.2). If the defender has played high side, 1 dribbles toward the baseline for a pass inside to 5 for the drop-step layup.

Strength can play an important part in gaining and maintaining position. In drill 3, if 1 has the ball and 5 can hold X5 high as the pass goes to 3, then 3 can pass into 5, who drop steps and shoots the power layup. 1, 3, and 5 must learn to read X5. 5 must learn to outmaneuver X5, using strength and leverage to control X5. 5 might even allow X5 to make a mistake and then not let X5 recover from it.

Positioning

Positioning consists of two parts—position on the floor and position on the defender.

To obtain proper positioning on the floor, low-post players race to the big block on the first possession down the floor. Where the defender plays the attacker determines where the low-post player will line up on all ensuing possessions. If the defender plays behind the post—this is suicide in modern basketball—the post player straddles the big block on all subsequent possessions. If the defender plays high side, the post moves up the lane to where the lead foot is just below the first small rectangle from the baseline. If the defender plays baseline or low side, the post attacker places the lead foot just below the big block. In this case the turnaround jumper on the baseline is not possible (the attacker would be behind the backboard), but the attacker would not use the jumper anyway when the defense plays below the low-post attacker. If the defender fronts, the low post moves away from the lane one step (about a foot to a foot and a half). Starting farther up or down the lane (three-quartering) or farther from the lane (fronting) would result in the defender altering his position, taking the advantage away from the offense. By beginning in this floor position the low-post player has already created a larger area for passes to come into the low post. It also gives more room to make a move to the basket after receiving the pass (figure 4.2).

There are only three basic defensive positions a defender can take on the low post. The defender can play behind, in front, or play high or low side in a three-quartering or less position. There are offensive maneuvers that all low-post players would want to use to establish position and then maintain it (leveraging) (figure 4.3). Let's take each defensive position one at a time.

Courtesy of University of Tennessee/Women's Sport Information

Figure 4.2   Daedra Charles (32) shows excellent offensive positioning. A pass inside could likely result in a drop step and a baby hook layup.

Begin with playing behind the low post. To successfully defend a strong-scoring low-post attacker from behind, a defender must receive plenty of help from the perimeter defenders. The low-post attacker would want to squat down a little more than usual. The attacker should hold up both hands as a target, hoping the defender will make contact coming over the attacker's back to deflect this pass, a common defensive mistake. The attacker would want to have his feet slightly farther than shoulder-width apart. He should straddle the big block. He wants to feel his defender with his buttocks. To maintain positioning, he moves as the defender moves. If

© NBA Photos/Fernando Medina

Figure 4.3   O'Neal establishes his position and maintains it using leverage.

the defender goes right, the attacker goes right, using quick slide steps. He should keep his weight on the foot away from where he feels the defender. This allows quicker foot movement.

Fronting is the second favorite defensive position. Some coaches, however, will front when the ball is low and three-quarter high side when the ball is high. Whenever the attacker is fronted, teammates of the low-post player should first clear the weak side. The low-post attacker should turn sideways to the fronting defender and put his elbow in the small of the defender's back. He holds up the hand away from the defender as a target. A flip lob pass comes in to the low post (see "The Pass"). As the flip lob comes in, the low-post player holds this position until the ball clears the top of the defensive player's head. As this happens, the offensive player releases, being careful not to push off, and goes to get the ball. The ball should never carry farther than one step away. In the case of the lob pass only, the attacker does not pull the pass in with elbows flared out. In this case, the attacker catches the ball and springs into the air in an immediate dive toward the basket for the power layup.

The favorite defensive position is three-quartering on the high or low side (usually the ball side). When this occurs, the attacker uses a wide stance with a low base (see figure 4.4). The attacker places the front foot at least equal to, and hopefully in front of, the defender's front foot. The low post bends at the knee and at the waist. This lowers the center of gravity, creating quicker foot movement. While establishing position, the attacker keeps his weight on the back foot. This allows the attacker to constantly slide his front foot outside. Once the low post has position, he should change his weight to his front foot. This allows him to constantly slide his back foot, moving as the defender moves (leverage). It also allows the low post to make the quick drop step if a pass comes inside. The attacker uses quick slide steps to keep this position. As the defender moves, the attacker moves. The attacker should bend the arm on the side of the defender at a 90-degree angle and place the lower arm on the defender anywhere from the upper leg to the lower torso. The attacker should keep the elbow close to the body to prevent pushing off. The lower arm should be stiffened, strengthening it. If the attacker has developed proper strength, this arm contact should prevent the defender from moving quickly to regain defensive positioning. The off hand should be used as a target hand.

Defensive team philosophy can also play an important part in positioning. Some coaches cut all perimeter players inside and three-quarter the low post high side; some do just the opposite—cut

© NBA Photos / Andrew Bernstein

Figure 4.4 David Robinson has perfect target hand positioning and is ready to receive the pass.

outside and three-quarter low side. There are almost as many defensive philosophies as there are coaches. A good scouting report or playing a few possessions at the beginning of the game usually reveals this philosophy. Wise players and coaches make use of this knowledge.

Zone defenders are easier to post up than man-to-man defenders. Zone defenders have the inside arm (arm away from goal) up. When attackers go across the lane, they should have both arms up. When they approach the zone defender, the attacker should have his arm higher than the shoulder of the defender. Attackers bring the goal-side arm down on top of the defender's arm. Perimeter passers, upon seeing the attacker's goal-side arm come down, should deliver the pass to the other arm (the target arm) of the attacker. The defender cannot get the inside arm to the ball to deflect it since the arm is pinned down. The defender cannot pivot to use the arm nearest the basket because of strength of the attacker's arm pressure. If the defender tries, the attacker has a layup. If the defender drops back to cover the basket, the low-post cutter has an easy turnaround jumper.

The best way to drill on proper position is to place the player on the big block. Put a defender in one of the four basic defensive positions. The low-post attacker immediately moves to the proper spot on the floor and places his body properly on his defender. The coach checks each point for correctness. Repeat this process several times each week. After the coach is content with correct positioning, the post-up or roll drill (drill 3) can be used to make posting live.

The Target

The off hand and arm, the one away from the defender, presents the target. The upper arm should be parallel to the floor and the lower arm perpendicular to the upper arm. Actually the angle at the elbow can be more than 90 degrees. The palm should be facing the passer, the fingers well spread and relaxed. A good drill to get the exact feel for the hand is for the player to spread the fingers until they hurt and then relax the fingers. This provides the exact spread and relaxation the hand and fingers should enjoy when presenting a target. Also, it provides a cup in the middle of the palm, making a softer hand that can more easily catch the ensuing pass.

Establish targets aggressively. Targets are maintained and protected through proper foot and body movement (see "Positioning").

Two results should be evident when proper teamwork is used on targeting. The inside player gives the target sign. The target is on the side where the attacker feels an opening. The perimeter passer checks this target area to be sure it is truly open. The inside player must make a sure and quick move as he receives the pass (see chapter 9). The situation may change quickly and radically after receiving the pass. That subject is considered under the section on moves.

The Pass

As a coach, I teach three passes to get the ball into the low post—the flip pass, the bounce pass, and the flip lob. The overhead flip lob is used against fronting defenders, the overhead flip against zone defenders, and the bounce pass when defenders play behind the low post or when the defender three-quarters on one side of the attacker. The bounce pass to the tall player is a great source of discussion among basketball coaches. Some say tall players don't handle it well. The tall player's hands, however, can be developed. Besides, the bounce pass, when thrown properly, comes up to the waist or letter area and tall players (as well as guards and forwards who post up) can easily handle this.

By mandating which pass to use in each situation, both the receiver and the passer will know where passes are coming from and where they are going. This eliminates many turnovers. Also, passers should always pass away from defenders, not directly to the post player.

Diagram 4.3 exhibits the only other possible passing impediment. X1 drops into the passing lane to help defense post player 5. In this situation 1 cannot get the ball inside to 5. So it is up to the passer to dribble and clear the passing lane. This always depends upon the position of the passer's defender. The passer must display good judgment. In the situation of diagram 4.3, 1 would dribble directly toward X1. 1 could now jump stop and make the pass inside to 5. Or 1 could cross over toward the baseline or the middle of the court. 5, upon seeing 1's drive, would drop step X5 and get body position. As X1 clears the passing lane to 5, 1 steps back and sidearms a bounce pass to 5 for the move and the shot or the pass back to 1 if X1 decides to double-down. 1 must make a good judgment, and 5 must read 1's intentions.

The Catch

Most tall players have poor hands. They fumble many easy passes. Usually they fumble passes because their hands are rigid and do not give with the reception. Fortunately, these steel hands can become soft hands with proper drilling and proper execution.

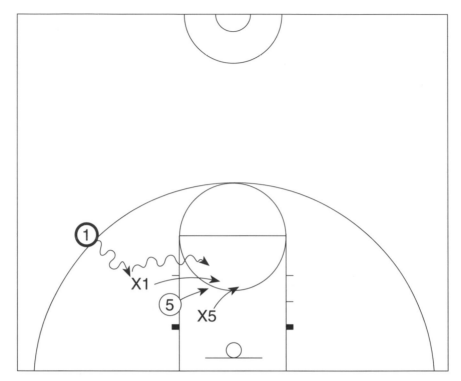

Diagram 4.3

The receiver should catch with both hands. The receiver should give a little as the ball hits the hand, which has been properly spread and cupped. The receiver should bring the second hand to the target hand as the ball hits the target hand. The receiver brings the ball to a position close to the body as she prepares to change from the catch to the move. This bringing of the ball close to the body and the move occur simultaneously. The receiver should spread the elbows outward with ball under the chin in a protected posture. The one exception to this is in receiving the lob pass. The lob pass should not be brought down; the ball should be held high and taken directly to the basket.

There are before-catch maneuvers that will help on the catch. The low post should face the teammate with the ball. Players in the post area should always have both hands up expecting a quick pass. Receivers should move in the direction of the pass, if possible. In all likelihood the passer has passed to the open spot (target) and the defender must move to stay with the low post. This means the low post will maintain positioning. When the post arrives at the catch, she wants to land on both feet (jump stop). This will give the low post two pivot feet, better balance, and more strength. An inadvertent bump won't cause the loss of the ball.

The low post should stay low if the defender is the same size or taller. Attackers should stay high if their defender is smaller, using this size advantage to receive and score. Using these two basic ideas allows the low post to protect any pass she receives.

Coaches can do many things to improve the low post's hands. Some have already been described in chapter 2. The pitcher's drill develops hand-eye coordination as well as soft hands. The toss ball off wall drill develops soft hands and quick moves off receiving the pass. The handgrippers, described in chapter 2, should be used religiously. I also use two full-court drills (drills 4 and 5) that improve not only ballhandling but also coordination, agility, running, and endurance. The quick growing, big player usually needs improvement in all these areas.

Inside players must be relentless in their desire to establish the correct floor position, the correct body position, and the catch of the pass. One hand will do to stop the ball, but both hands must be used to keep the pass from falling to the floor.

The Move

Now that the ball is at the low-post position, the attacker must make a move to score. As in all phases of the attack, maintain simplicity and logic. The moves system should follow that philosophy. Post players begin by learning two primary moves—the drop step (back-to-basket moves) and the turnaround (face-up moves). The drop step includes the drop step baseline and drop step middle. The turnaround is similarly divided into the turnaround baseline and turnaround middle. After the post players have mastered these primary moves, they can move to the basic four. The primary two and the basic four constitute the fundamental moves system. More advanced moves, which fit perfectly and logically into this fundamental moves system, are offered in chapter 9 for the more developed player.

Players must develop their moves system slowly. They must learn the primary two before attempting the basic four. Patience is important here. Make sure of the drop step and the turnaround before attempting the spin, the half-spin, or the face-up moves.

First, consider the drop step. If you drop step baseline, slide dribble, if needed, and end with a power layup. If you drop step inside, slide dribble, if needed, and end with either the hook layin or the turnaround jumper.

The drop step, diagram 4.4, begins before the pass comes into the post. It starts with proper positioning on the defender. As the pass enters the low-post region, the low post drops his foot back (reverse pivots) so the attacker can feel his new lead foot hook the defender's back foot. Some attackers wait to receive the pass before drop stepping. This allows the defender to recover. Other attackers will leave too soon, allowing the defender to step in and steal the pass. Proper timing is critical. Drilling and hard work will overcome these mistakes. The attacker wants to put the lead elbow on the backside of his defender, but he does not want to hold or push or hook with it. The low post uses his elbow to determine if he has successfully drop stepped his defender. If the attacker needs to regain balance or if the distance from the beginning of the move to the basket requires it, the drop-stepping low post uses one slide dribble. If the drop step was baseline, the attacker should now have turned toward the basket and should have his body between the defender and the basket.

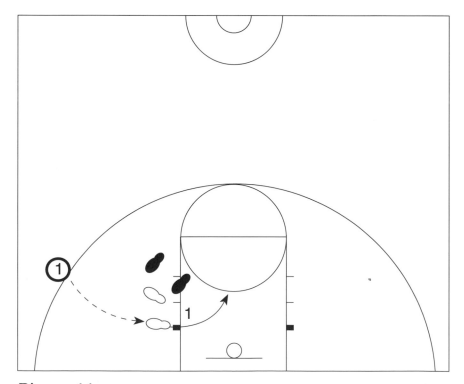

Diagram 4.4

If the drop step was middle, the body of the attacker should be pointing toward the basket for the hook layin or turnaround jumper. Anytime the low post sees the shoulder of the defender (or a help defender) after he starts the drop step, he should immediately consider another move option.

The attacker uses a drop step when a defender three-quarters on the high or low side. This leaves a direct route to the basket after the drop step. Also, when a defender plays behind but tight on the attacker, the low post can quickly show the ball opposite the direction he intends to drop step or turnaround.

This showing of the ball must look like a move in that direction, but the feet must stay glued to the floor. Otherwise, the attacker will walk on this move. The attacker shows the ball just above the shoulder, say the right shoulder, and turns his head to the right. The attacker's eyes should glance down at the defender's feet, studying where the defender is located. If the defender stays directly behind the attacker or moves in the direction of the fake, the attacker should drop the left foot to hook the defender's left foot, and the drop step is on. Shaquille O'Neal is a master at making this move.

What if the defender is shading the attacker's left side while playing behind the low post? The drop step can still be used. As the attacker shows the ball over his right shoulder and glances at the defender's feet, he sees this overplay to the left side. Because the attacker, even on the ball fake, keeps both feet on the floor, he still has both feet as pivot feet. The attacker drops his right foot, hooking the defender's right foot, and the drop step is on.

Anytime a drop step is used, the attacker might find himself too far from the basket to power the muscle shot. The attacker can then use a slide-step dribble to get near the basket for the muscle shot (power layup). Beginning post players sometimes perform a successful drop step but then leave their shoulders perpendicular to the basket instead of parallel. Be patient: it takes time to develop a good drop-step sequence.

Should the attacker begin his drop step erroneously (misread the defense), he will quickly see the trail shoulder of the defender. To continue the move will result in a charge. This sets up the four basic moves. The attacker must recognize and must immediately consider one of the basic four—the crossover, the spin, the pump fake, or the half-spin.

When using the ball fake and glance, the low-post player may see the defender back off. If so, the attacker no longer has the drop step. So the attacker uses the face-up moves or the turnarounds. The moves are designed to put the defense at a disadvantage and to allow the offense to seize the opportunity to move and score. Players must be able not only to execute the move at an accelerated pace but also to make good judgment of when to use that move. All of this can be learned.

The turnaround baseline and turnaround middle are simple turnaround reverse pivots (turnaround baseline is shown in diagram 4.5). The pivot must be a complete 180 degrees. By turning the full 180 degrees, the low-post player is squared to the basket for the jump shot, and the front foot comes directly toward the basket, forcing the defender to get between the attacker and the basket. This movement by the defense sets up the crossover moves.

The step-through or crossover is the first basic move. It is a counter to the turnarounds. After the turnaround, say baseline, the low-post player has moved away from the defender (see figure 4.5). The jump shot is readily available. After hitting a few jump shots off the turnaround (see "The Shot"), the defender will usually step toward the

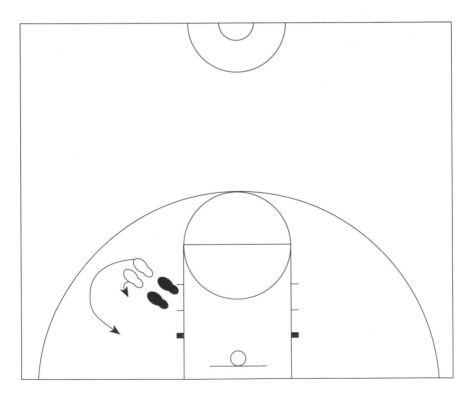

Diagram 4.5

© NBA Photos/Andrew Bernstein

Figure 4.5 Charles Barkley exposes the ball to his right as he glances over his left shoulder to check defensive positioning.

shooter. When this happens, the low post crosses his baseline foot over between the defender and himself. If needed, the low post takes one dribble. He now is in the same position as he was on the drop step middle. He is ready to shoot the hook layin.

The next basic move is the spin. The spin is best shown using the drop step, spin, hook layin (if going to the middle—diagrams 4.6 and 4.7) and drop step, spin, power layup (if going baseline). I'll describe the mechanics of the drop step, spin, hook layin (both moves are identical—one begins with the drop step baseline and the other with the drop step middle). The same sequence can be executed using the turnaround (face-up), crossover, spin, power layup. All the moves fit comfortably with each other. The shot that is executed depends on where the move ends up—in the middle, the hook; on the baseline, the power layup.

To execute the drop step baseline, spin, hook layin, the low post begins with a basic drop step baseline. When he sees the inside shoulder of his defender, the low post knows the power layup is not available (in high school basketball a charging foul eliminates the field goal).

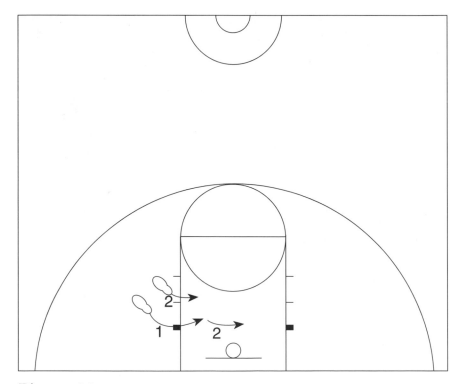

Diagram 4.6

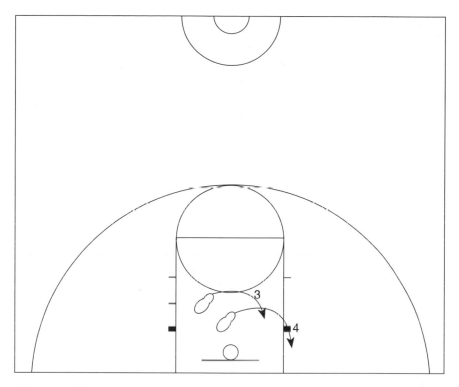

Diagram 4.7

The low post should pick up his dribble and pump fake. If he gets his defender in the air, he can dive toward the basket for a power layup. Or the low post can drop step, see the defender's shoulder, spin (actually another drop step, reverse pivot—see diagram 4.7) while he takes one dribble toward the middle, and shoot the hook layin.

The last basic move is the half-spin. The half-spin comes after either the drop step or the turnaround crossover. It, too, is interchangeable with the others. They all fit comfortably with each other, giving the creative post player unlimited fakes. The half-spin is the counter to the drop step, spin, hook layin or power layup. The half-spin is exactly what it says. The low post spins (actually does a second drop step) but pivots 180 degrees back to face the basket. For example, the low post drop steps baseline, sees his opponent's inside shoulder, and picks up his dribble as he spins to the middle. But when his lead foot hits the floor, he reverse pivots all the way back 180 degrees. Now he has the power layup (from diagrams 4.7 to 4.8). Hakeem Olajuwon has perfected both the spin and half-spin moves (see figure 4.6).

© NBA Photos/Barry Gossage

Figure 4.6   Hakeem Olajuwon begins a spin move to his left after Shaquille O'Neal cuts him off.

KEY COACHING POINTS

The Primary and Basic Moves

The primary two are the drop step and the turnaround. The drop step occurs with the back to the basket. The attacker faces the basket for the turnaround; hence, it is called a face-up move.

The turnaround is used under two conditions. The post player can simply receive the pass, turn around with a reverse pivot, and shoot the jump shot. The second condition is when the post player tries to use the turnaround to induce his defender into a mistake. He does this by keeping both feet planted on the floor and glancing toward the feet of the defender while exposing the ball over his shoulder. The post player reads how the defender reacts to this fake and either drop steps (to one side or the other) or turns around.

The basic four are the pump fake, the spin, the half-spin, and the crossover. All are interchangeable and may be used at anytime during any move.

Pump fakes are used after the attacker picks up the ball and wants to get the defender off balance. At the end of a dribble, the post player pump fakes, gets the defender off balance, and shoots the power layup. Or, the attacker turns around, pump fakes, gets the defender off balance, and crosses over (or drives directly to the basket). These are just two of the infinite uses of this moves system. A player has to learn only the primary two and the basic four and he has an unlimited number of fakes.

The attacker uses spins to move far away from the defender. A spin usually moves the attacker from one side of the basket to the other, creating separation from a defender and an easy shot. This move is available always, even while executing another primary or basic move.

The attacker uses half-spins to create deception from the full spin. While the full spin takes the attacker to the other side of the basket, the half-spin keeps the attacker on the same side of the basket. Like the spin, it creates separation and an easy shot. It, too, is interchangeable and may be used during any primary or basic move.

The crossover, and its kindred—the direct drive—is used mainly after a face-up (the turnaround). Like the drop step, the crossover gets the defense in motion, causing a defensive mistake. Even if the defender uses the correct coverage, the attacker can immediately exploit it with the spin, the half-spin, the pump fake, the drop step, or another turnaround off the dribble. All are available, all are interchangeable; the player can learn each separately, and use them as independent, single moves. That is the beauty of this moves system.

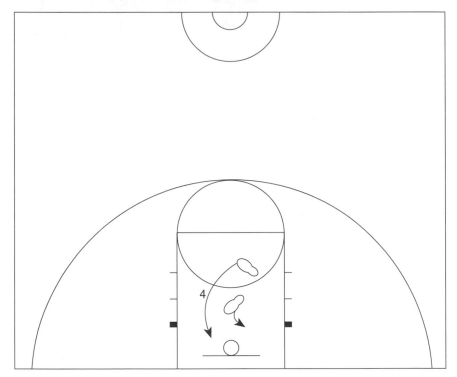

Diagram 4.8

The last five diagrams in this section show the drop step (diagram 4.9), the turnaround (diagram 4.10), the face-ups (the crossover and the direct drive; diagram 4.11), the spin (diagram 4.12), and the half-spin (diagram 4.13).

With the primary two and the basic four, a low post can create moves by using combinations. But don't let your low post become too creative. Simple is best.

Here are two combinations your low post can use. The low-post player uses the turnaround baseline and pump fakes to get the defender to jump at her. When the defender jumps, the attacker crosses over to the middle, half-spins back toward the baseline and then back to the middle for a hook layin.

For variation the low-post player uses the turnaround baseline, pump fakes, crosses over to the middle, and then spins back to the baseline for a power layup. Encourage your post players to practice combinations; it will make them more mobile around the basket. But when game time comes keep it simple.

The DeVoe drill is best for inspecting and correcting fakes. The attacker tosses the ball out in front of herself with a backspin so that it will come back to her. She catches the ball with two hands as she jump stops. The attacker then makes a move. This drill allows the coach to correct mechanical flaws and permits a low-post candidate to practice alone in the off-season.

This is another good drill. The coach has the ball, and the player flashes to the ball. The coach tells a defender to play above, below, front, or behind. The attacker must recognize the defense and make the correct choice of positioning and move. If played at either of the three-quartering positions (high or low), the attacker would start with the drop step. If played behind, the attacker would use either of two turnarounds (preferably baseline) or fake, showing the ball in one direction and drop stepping in the other. If fronted, the attacker would receive the lob pass and use the muscle shot.

Drill 3 offers a chance to go live. 1 passes to 3, and 5 uses his guile to get open. As the pass comes into 5, he must by feel or sight know where X5 is. 5 immediately makes the correct move. As you will see in the section on savvy, this is the first of the building-block drills (see "The Savvy—Knowing When").

Low-post players should learn the moves in the following order.

Primary Moves

1. Drop steps (baseline and middle)—back-to-basket moves.
2. Turnarounds (baseline and middle)—known as face-up moves.

Before going on, players should master the primary moves. This requires patience.

Basic Moves

1. Crossover (or direct drive). This move is used after the player executes the turnaround.

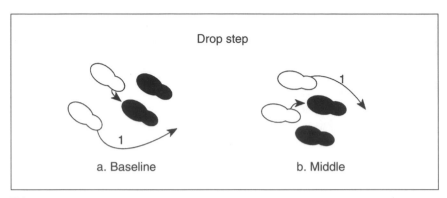

Diagram 4.9

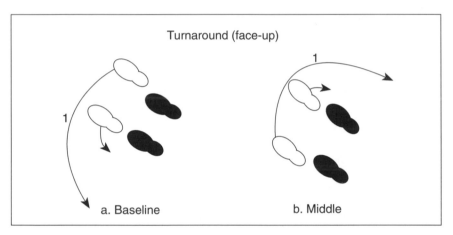

Diagram 4.10

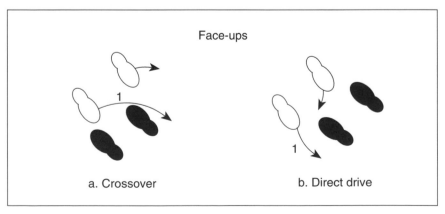

Diagram 4.11

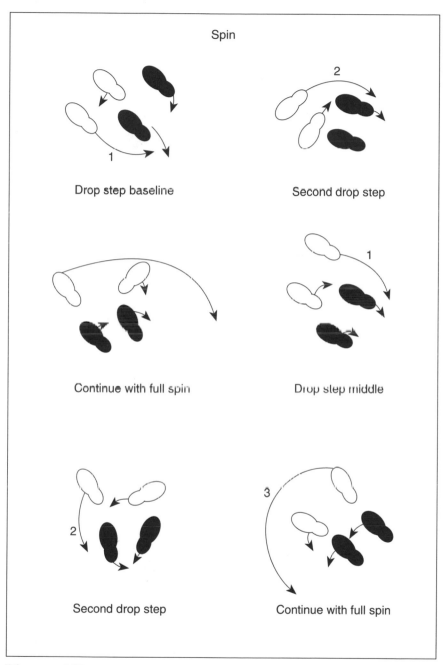

Diagram 4.12

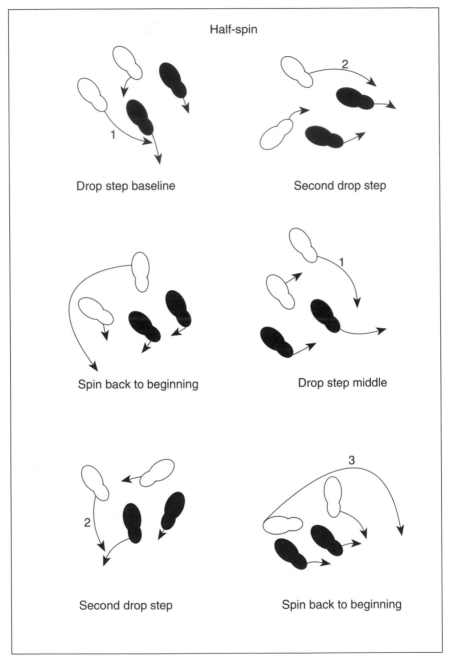

Diagram 4.13

2. Spin. This move occurs from either the crossover, the drop step, or the half-spin.
3. Half-spin. This move develops from either the crossover, the drop step, or the spin.
4. Pump fake. This move occurs at any time during the fakes of any move or at the end of any move.

After learning the basic moves, the player has a complete moves system. The low-post attacker can now put together unlimited combinations of moves, such as drop step baseline, half-spin, pump fake, then crossover. The combinations are infinite, limited only by the imagination of the low-post attacker.

Now the low-post attacker is ready to learn the advanced moves of chapter 9. The moves in chapter 9 work perfectly with the primary and basic moves, and a new set of combinations can be created.

The Shot

All the moves—primary, basic, and advanced—end in one of four types of shots. These are the turnaround jump shot, the power layup (sometimes called the muscle shot), the hook layin, and the pump fake (not really a shot, but the end of many moves).

The turnaround jump shot is the basic jump shot used by perimeter players. The ball is held in front, brought up through a shooting pocket, and flipped toward the goal—a regular jump shot. It is best to require that the shot be banked off the board. A spot slightly outside the rectangle is perfect for the bank. It should hit this spot on the way down from its arc. Anyone, even the 6-foot-6 defensive tackle discussed earlier, can hit this shot with a high percentage. It is easily learned and highly effective.

The attacker shoots the power layup at the end of a drop step, spin, or half-spin, or after an offensive rebound. To complete it successfully, the low-post player needs to bow the neck. This makes him stronger. The attacker brings the ball to a hitched position with arms at a 45-degree angle and forearms tensed. He holds the ball very tightly. The shot starts over the shoulder away from the defender. The attacker explodes into the air with a slight body lean into the defender. It is not a high jump; it is a dive toward the basket. This shot is placed high and easy on the glass. The higher the shot is banked on the glass, the better the chance it will go in even if the shooter is fouled.

The only other shot to teach is the hook layin. It is simply a short hook laid in over the rim (see figure 4.7). A slight flip of the wrist after the ball is over the rim scores the basket. Use a variation of the Mikan drill (Hook Layin Drill, drill 6) to teach it and to constantly drill it.

The pump fake is not really a shot, but it can be used at the end of any move to set up another move. It is used to get defenders into the air and out of position to stop the ensuing move. To be effective, the pump fake must look exactly like a shot (the power layup or the turnaround jumper). The attacker should have his knees bent and his rear extended. He should fake the shot by showing the ball to the defender. The attacker should have his arms fully extended overhead, and his feet should remain glued to the floor. The attacker should be ready to shoot and maybe move into the defender, once the defender leaves the floor or even comes up on his toes.

The pump fake and the power layup are both taught using the same drill (drill 7).

Work daily on the moves and shots with individual drills and this team drill—the three-man posting drill (drill 8).

The Savvy—Knowing When

I have discussed what maneuvers to perform and how to do them. Now you are ready to learn when to use these strategies. I teach "when" with a series of progressive drills.

Defense can play a low post one-on-one if they wish. They can cover by three-quartering, by playing behind the attacker, or by fronting. Or they can combine several of these. A popular coverage today is to cover the high side of the attacker (three-quartering) when the ball is high and to front when the ball is low.

Defense also makes use of team maneuvers when the ball reaches the low post. The basic three are

- double-down from strong side,
- double-down from weak side, and
- rotate from weak side.

Drill using the probable defense of your next opponent. During the year cover the basic three many times. And drill often against your own defensive strategies. Teach the defense while teaching the offense so that your practices will be at least equal to any game situation. For more detail on how to teach the defense, see chapter 8.

Figure 4.7   Using his left arm perfectly for protection, O'Neal shoots a dip shot over Robinson.

The post-up or roll drill (drills 9 and 10) begins the teaching of when. In these drills, 5 must make quick one-on-one decisions. Some teams still try to prevent the low post from scoring by using only one-on-one defensive tactics, but the number dwindles every year. Some coaches say that with the explosive use of the three-point perimeter shot, one-on-one coverage will again become popular.

HIGH- AND MID-POST FAKES

Every low-post fake is equally effective from the high post. The same theory of scoring is also in effect: Make the first move in direction of the pass (see chapter 9, "Post Scoring Theory"). To the combination of fakes presented in diagrams 4.11, 4.12, and 4.13, add only the rocker-step series. I'll first discuss all the low-post fakes from the high post before covering the rocker-step series.

Diagram 4.14 shows the drop step from the high post. 1 passes away from the defender, X5, as 5 cuts to the high post. 5 immediately drop steps and drives to the basket for a layup using only one dribble. 5 lays the dribble out front, keeping her body between the ball and X5, leaping high and toward basket for a left-handed layup.

If X5 recovers, or 5 misreads X5, or 5 sees the outside shoulder of another defender coming to help, then 5 must consider another move. What moves are available? The attacker can use the spin or half-spin, can pick up the dribble and pump fake for the jump shot, or can use the crossover at end of any of these moves. In other words, any option that was available at the low post is also available at the high or mid post. To this, add the rocker-step series.

Rocker-Step Series

Face-up moves are available when the high post receives the pass. The high post is usually defended from behind, not three-quartered or fronted. In fact, most teams have an automatic call—when fronted at the high post, throw the flip lob. There is no defensive help for any defender who fronts the high post. Because almost all defenders play behind the high post, the attacker should immediately reverse pivot upon receiving the ball. The reverse pivot is favored over the front pivot because it has the deception of greater movement

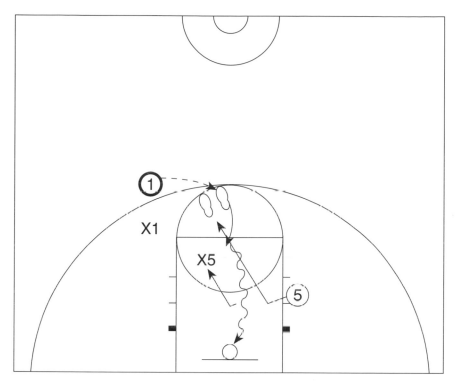

Diagram 4.14

away from the defender (diagram 4.15). As the attacker reverse pivots, she should keep the ball in a high overhead position, quickly
bringing the ball to a triple-threat position as she completes the turn.
This forces the defender into movement to stop the turnaround jump
shot.

As the high post pivots, she should check over her shoulder to
see the defensive posture of her defender. This checking should allow the high post to determine quickly whether she should pump
fake and drive or shoot the direct jumper.

Without proper defensive footwork, the high post may have a
direct drive to the basket. (In diagram 4.15, the attacker places her
right foot beside the defender's left foot—a long stride step—and
takes a one-dribble drive to the basket, protecting the ball with the
body.) If the defender overreacts to the initial reverse pivot, the high
post crossover steps (diagram 4.16) and takes a one-dribble drive to
her left for a left-handed layup.

Upon reverse pivoting, if the high-post defender does not come
to a tight coverage, the high-post attacker can shoot the immediate

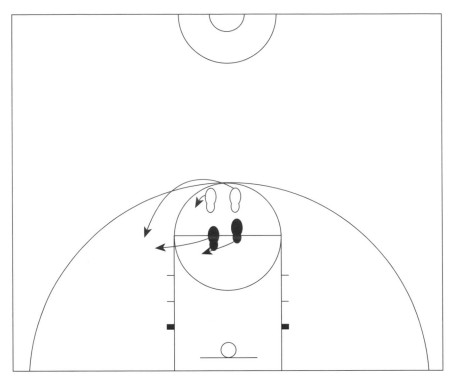

Diagram 4.15

jump shot. Or the high-post attacker can compel the defender to move toward her by pump faking the jump shot. As the high-post attacker pump fakes the jump shot, she should head fake and shoulder fake by throwing the head and shoulders back and up. This makes the defender move up onto the attacker to stop the threat of the jump shot. Now the direct drive or the crossover is again available. This pump fake of the jump shot is another illustration of forcing the defender into a mistake and not letting her recover. Once the drive begins, if the attacker sees a defender's shoulder, the attacker must consider another move—the spin, the half-spin, the pump fake, or another crossover at the end of the dribble.

All the above are part of the rocker step (a face-up move). One more technique must be added to complete the rocker-step series. The attacker can jab step toward the defender. In diagram 4.16, the attacker jabs her right foot beside the defender's left foot. The attacker stays on her toes but shifts her weight backward. The attacker fakes her head and shoulders in a movement upward and backward as if she intends to shoot the jump shot. The attacker may even bring

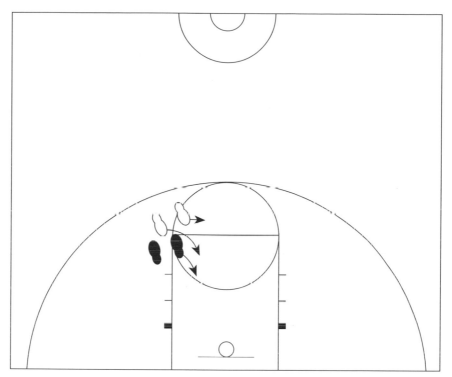

Diagram 4.16

the ball up through the shooting pocket. As the defender lunges forward to stop this jump-shot threat, the attacker straight drives or crossover drives (whichever the defender gives) to the basket. If the attacker sees the opponent's shoulder as she begins her drive, she should immediately consider another move.

A complement to the direct jab is the crossover jab. After the reverse pivot (face-up), the attacker crosses her right foot beside the right foot of the defender (diagram 4.16). No reaction by the defender would give the attacker a drive to the basket. A reaction by the defender starts the attacker on a full spin and drive to the basket.

Diagram 4.15 illustrates the rocker-step series with a pivot on the left foot. The attacker could have pivoted on the right foot and made the rocker step in the other direction.

All cuts to the high post should end in a jump stop. This minimizes any chance of an interception and enables the high post to pivot on either foot. The high post should immediately pivot to face the basket or should immediately drive with a drop step. This reception should be from a crouched position with head up, tail down, back bent slightly forward, arms outstretched, and feet in a parallel position. Upon receiving the ball, the high post should extend the elbows out parallel to the floor to protect the ball. Should the high post decide to drive with the ball, the first step should be long and quick, enabling the high post to elude the defender. This long step must give the high-post attacker at least a half step on her defender. As she drives, the high post protects the ball with the arm not being used to dribble. If the high post gets the layup, she would want to extend her shooting arm slightly forward and away from the defender. The high post should jump high and toward the basket.

When the high post squares up toward the basket after receiving the ball, she should keep the ball low and off her hips if there is no help defender around. This gives the threat of a drive, enabling the high post to pass or shoot the jump shot more easily.

The high post will make more use of the slide-step dribble than the low post. Anytime the high post begins a move toward the basket and has to change her move because of good defense, she should use the slide-step dribble. Or the high post can begin the drive with a power dribble. In either case the high post wants to land on both feet with the last dribble. This gives the high-post driver either foot as a pivot foot for the turnaround jumper or another move at the end of the dribble. When the high post sees a direct route to the basket, she should use an explosive power dribble. She should use a slide-step dribble in all other cases.

If the high post is facing a zone or if the high post intends to pass, she should bring the ball overhead with arms extended as she receives the ball. This protects the ball from help defenders and allows for a quicker pass. The high post must develop the ability to look through her defender to the low post to pass the high-low pass, to shoot, or to drive.

On any face-up move, if the high post can get her shoulder beside the defender, she should continue aggressively toward the basket. If the high post sees that the defender's shoulder is ahead, she should consider a spin, a half-spin, a jump shot, or a pass.

Beginning in and staying in a low, crouched position enables the high post to move quicker, maintain better body balance, and stop suddenly without charging into the defender or committing another violation.

With her back to a defender, the high post should keep her rear end out, and arms and hands extended outward (with or without ball). She wants to be able to pivot freely and quickly, to react instantaneously to her defender's position (diagrams 4.17, 4.18, 4.19,

4.20, and 4.21). Hopefully, the high post will not be in this position often.

Summary of High-Post Movement

1. The high post should immediately drive if it is available (use the drop step).
2. If the drop step is not available, the high post should pivot and face the defense (keep tail low, head up, knees bent, primed to spring forward for the jump shot).
3. If, as the high post pivots, the defense comes in tight, the high post should dip the shoulder, take the big first step, and go for the layup, using only one (power) dribble.
4. If, as the high post pivots, the defense stays loose, the high post should take the jump shot.

The key is to recognize immediately the position of the defense. The high post can obtain this information by looking over her shoul-

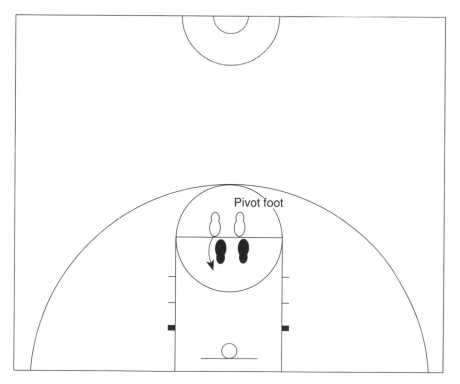

Diagram 4.17

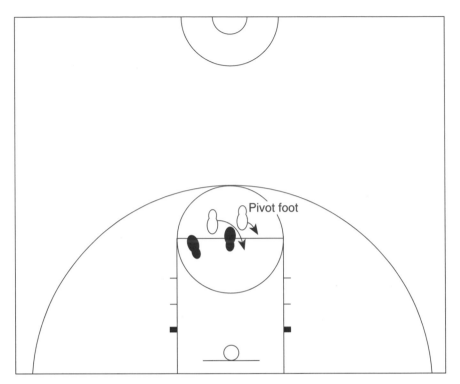

Diagram 4.18

der as she pivots. High-post players must learn to recognize which foot of the defender is forward, how far forward it is, and whether it is right or left of the potential high-post pivot foot (the direction of the high-post pivot will determine the pivot foot).

Diagram 4.17 shows the nonpivot foot being placed outside the defender's foot. The high post would drive right. This occurs when the defender's foot is inside the body of the high-post attacker. If the defender overshifted, diagram 4.18 displays the crossover and drive left. If the defender plays straight and tight, the attacker would pump fake and then drive on whichever defensive foot came forward (diagram 4.19). Diagram 4.20 exhibits the left defensive pivot foot coming forward but not outside the attacker's body. A direct drive resulted. Diagram 4.21 shows the crossover being used because the defender's right foot came forward.

If the coach uses a high-low set offense, the low post must learn to clear the side where the high post is driving. If that low post's defender stays, the high post can pass off to the clearing low post for a layup.

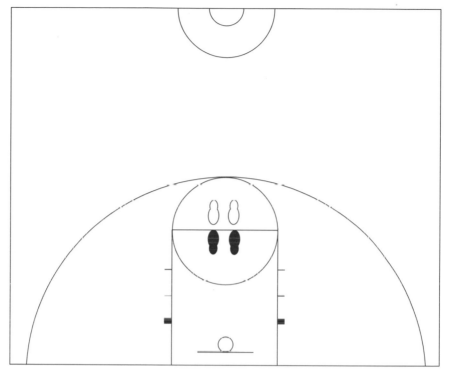

Diagram 4.19

The reverse pivot has the illusion of creating greater space from the defender. The front pivot often freezes the defender where he is. So the reverse pivot compels the defender to shift at least half a man. This defensive shift provides the attacker with a golden opportunity to drive while the defender is moving.

SKILLS WRAP-UP

Scoring is every basketball player's dream. Players need to know how to get open, how to help themselves receive a pass, how to make a move after getting the ball, and how to shoot after getting the ball. They also need to know when to do these things so that scores result.

Primary fakes and basic fakes from the low post are developed. They are interchangeable, leading to an infinite variety of fakes, known as combinations. High-post fakes, including the rocker-step series, conclude the scoring options.

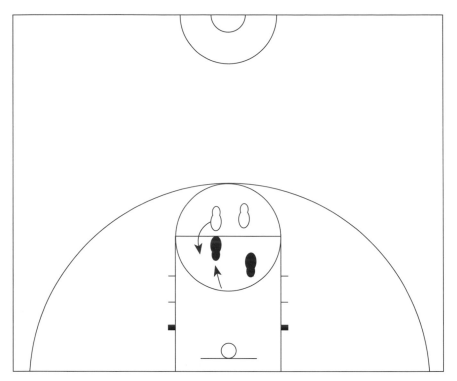

Diagram 4.20

Suppose, after doing all these steps correctly, that the shot is missed. Someone has to go get the rebound. That is the subject of chapter 5.

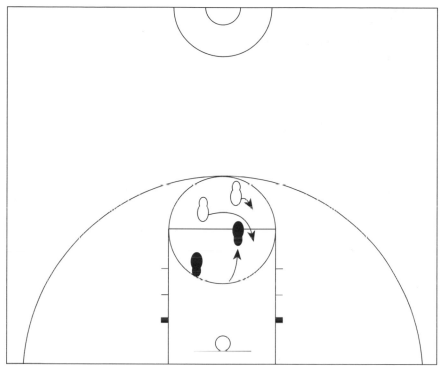

Diagram 4.21

3 Roll Drill

Objectives

1. To learn posting up.
2. To learn the roll.
3. To learn proper defense of the big block area.
4. To learn avoiding the pin.
5. To learn reading the defender, making a move, and scoring.
6. To learn cutting maneuvers from the strong side or the weak side. Coaches can decree the defense to play in a particular defensive position (fronting, for example) or a combination (three-quartering on the strong side when ball is high; fronting when ball is low).

Procedure

1. Line up post players out of bounds or on the weak-side block if you want to have them cut.
2. X5 begins on defense and 5 on offense. 1 and 3 can be coaches, post players, or perimeter players.
3. Rotate from offense, to defense, to end of the line. As 1 passes to 3, X5 tries to prevent 5 from getting position. 5 uses proper post-up techniques and uses the roll if the defense has the better position.
4. When 1 or 3 gets the ball inside to 5, 5 uses a quick move and a shot, the one dictated by the defender.
5. Before teaching offense with this drill, teach the defense how to defend the big block and how to avoid the pin (see chapter 8). You want your defense to be better than any you face all year. This enables your attackers to develop more quickly and with a sharper edge.

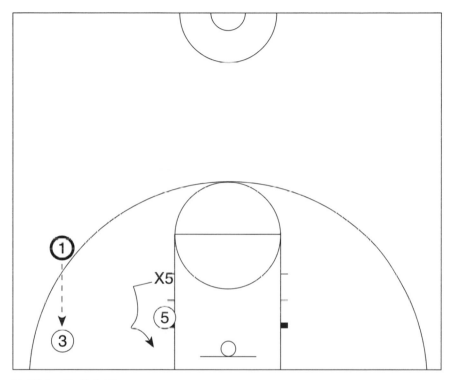

Drill 3   Roll drill.

4 Big Man's Fast-Break Drill

Objectives

1. To drill to develop soft hands.
2. To condition.
3. To help on coordination, agility, running, and endurance.

Procedure (steps are same as numbers in the diagram)

1. The post passes the ball to the coach and starts running up the side court.
2. The coach throws a bad pass to the post player—at the feet, at one side or the other, or high. The post player has to catch the ball.
3. The post passes the ball back to the coach and sprints up the floor.
4. The coach throws a lead pass to the post.
5. The post dribbles for a layup and rebounds the shot.
6. The post passes to the coach and starts running up court.
7. The coach throws a bad pass to the post by rolling it, throwing it at feet, to the side, or high. The post must catch the ball without fumbling it.
8. The post player throws the ball back to the coach and sprints up the floor.
9. The coach throws a lead pass that the post runs under.
10. The post drives for a layup, rebounds the shot, and the drill continues.

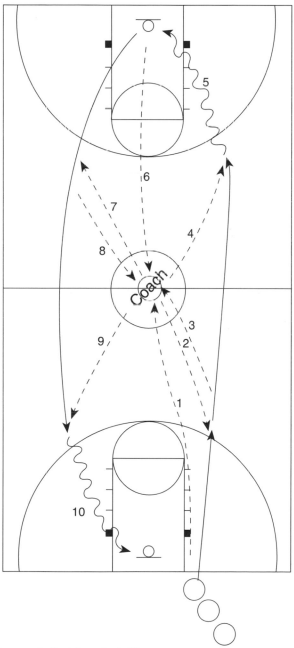

Drill 4   Big man's fast-break drill.

5 Run Full Court Well Drill

Objectives

1. To drill post players to run the court well.
2. To develop soft hands and good passing.
3. To condition.
4. To work on agility, running, and endurance.

Procedure

1. Line up post candidates at end court.
2. 4 passes to 1 to start drill. Meanwhile 5 has begun running. 1 passes to 5.
3. Meanwhile 4 has to really sprint. 5, upon receiving the pass, throws to 6.
4. 6 pivots and bounce passes to the sprinting 4, who must catch ball cleanly and lay it in using one motion.
5. Meanwhile 5 sprints and rebounds 4's shot (made or missed). 4 goes outside and sprints down court. 5 passes to 6 and the drill continues down the other side.
6. 6 passes to 4.
7. 4 passes to 1.
8. 1 passes to 5 for a layup. You could have two or more players in line to step out or you could require 4 and 5 to continue down and back again.

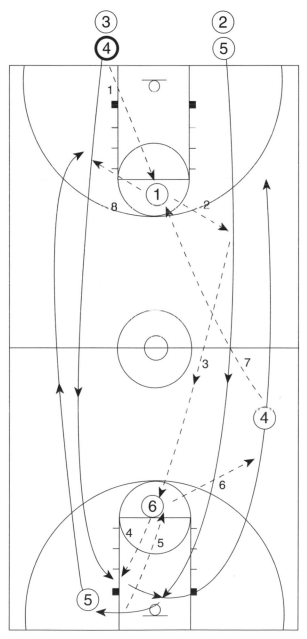

Drill 5   Run full court well drill.

6 Hook Layin Drill (The Mikan Drill)

Objectives

1. To drill the hook layin.
2. To drill coordination and agility.
3. To drill the drop step inside.
4. To drill the jump stop.
5. To condition.

Procedure

1. 5 drop steps inside and shoots baby hook layin over the rim. 5 rebounds his shot, tosses the ball out with backspin, and jumps toward the other big block, landing on both feet in a jump stop.
2. 5 immediately drop steps inside, shoots baby hook layin over the rim. 5 rebounds his shot, lands, tosses the ball out with backspin, and jumps toward his original big block, landing on both feet in a jump stop.
3. This continues for 30 seconds. As the season progresses, increase the time to one minute.

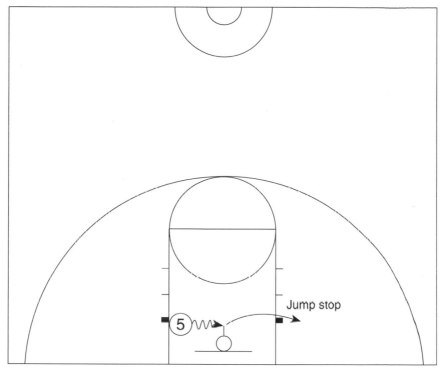

Drill 6   Hook layin drill.

7 Power Pick-Up Drill

Objectives

1. To drill the power layup.
2. To drill the pump fake.

Procedure

1. Line up a post player, 4, and a helper, 5. Two balls are used; one starts on each big block.
2. 4 races over to pick up one ball, drop steps, and shoots a power layup. 5 recovers the ball while 4 races to the other big block. 4 picks up this second ball, drop steps, and shoots a power layup. By now 5 has replaced the first ball and goes to retrieve the second ball. 5 replaces the second ball while 4 goes to get the first one. 4 continues this for 30 seconds before the two exchange duties.
3. Instead of 4 picking up the ball, drop stepping, and shooting a power layup, 4 can pick up the ball, drop step, pump fake, and shoot a power layup.
4. I do not recommend more than two pump fakes, preferably one. More than two always results in a three-second call.

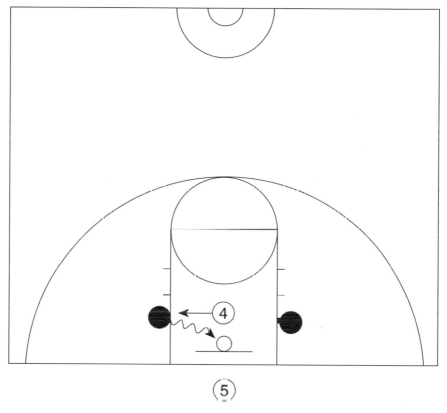

Drill 7   Power pick-up drill.

8 Three-Man Posting Drill

Objectives

1. To drill moves and shots.
2. To work on cuts across the lane (pretend the ball is high or low and get proper position on floor and defender).
3. To condition for the continuous play demanded at the low-post position.

Procedure

1. Both 3 and 4 have a basketball. 5 begins the drill by breaking toward 4. 4 throws pass to 5. 5 does the move the three are working on—for example, the drop step baseline and power layup.
2. 5 retrieves his shot and replaces 4. Meanwhile 4 breaks toward 3. 3 passes to 4 who does the prescribed move. 4 rebounds his shot and replaces 3. 3 has meanwhile cut across the lane toward 5 to receive his pass from 5 and make his move. The drill is continuous.
3. At the beginning of the season run this drill until players have mastered the moves. As the season progresses, the coach can begin to run this drill as a conditioning aid; start with three minutes and build up to eight.

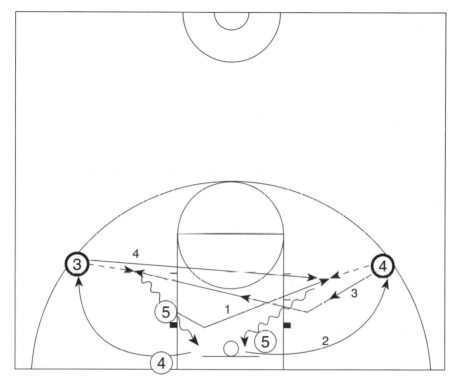

Drill 8   Three-man posting drill.

9 **Live Posting With Helper**

Objectives

1. To drill 5 to make a quick move using accurate judgment about X5's defense.
2. To drill X5 to cover the big block correctly, including avoiding the pin (see chapter 8).
3. To drill X4 to rotate to help.
4. To drill 5 to always expect defense help when 5 gets the ball at a low-post position (a basic principle covered in chapter 3).
5. To drill 5 on proper cutting techniques to get open.

Procedure

1. 5 tries to get position on X5 so 1 or 3 can pass ball inside. 5 uses all the techniques discussed in the sections on getting open and positioning.
2. X4 comes to help X5 when 5 receives the ball. X4 begins slightly on the weak side of the basket. 5 makes the move dictated by the defense of X5. If 5 uses bad judgment, the coach must correct him. X4 cannot move until 5 receives the pass.
3. 5 could break across lane if the coach wants to work on weak-side to strong-side cuts.

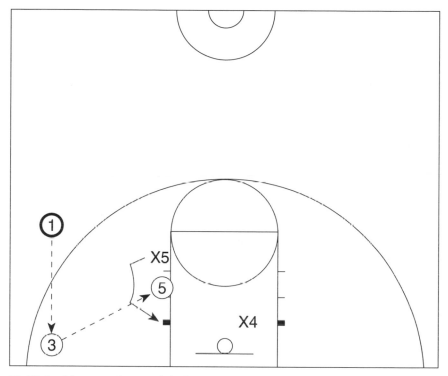

Drill 9   Live posting with helper drill.

10 Live Posting With Offensive Helper

Objectives

1. Same as live posting with helper drill, except it also drills 5 to pass from low post to low post (see chapter 6).
2. It also drills 4 to step toward the goal to get proper position for the pass from 5 or for a rebound should 5 shoot.
3. It teaches X4 to decide to rotate or to hedge (see chapter 8).

Procedure

1. Same procedure as live posting with helper drill, except this time X4 has an attacker he must guard.
2. If X4 rotates across to help X5 on 5, 5 must recognize this and pass off to 4. 4 should move to the basket.
3. X4 can hedge and then get back to his man, 4. 5 must recognize this and take the shot himself (see chapter 8, "Hedging").

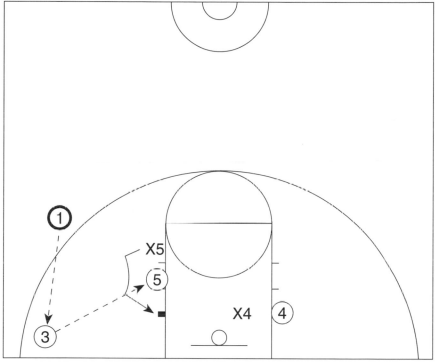

Drill 10   Live posting with offensive helper drill.

11 Rotation Drill

Objectives

1. To drill scoring moves, shots, and passing (see chapter 6).
2. To drill proper defensive rotations (see chapter 8).
3. To teach the weak-side attacker proper maneuvers to use against rotation of defenses.

Procedure

1. 1 and 2 pass the ball until they can get the ball inside to 4 or 5. Or, if the coach intends to post up guards, 1 and 2 can pass and screen down. This makes 1, 2, 4, and 5 all post-up candidates.
2. Once ball goes inside, to 5 in diagram, 5 makes move to the basket by drop stepping baseline.
3. Rotation begins the moment 5 starts to basket or when X4 sees 5 has potential for the power layup. X4 calls "rotate." This compels the weak-side guard, X2, to drop to cover the basket area. 4 should step toward the basket for a pass from 5. 2 should step in toward the basket, pressuring the defense.

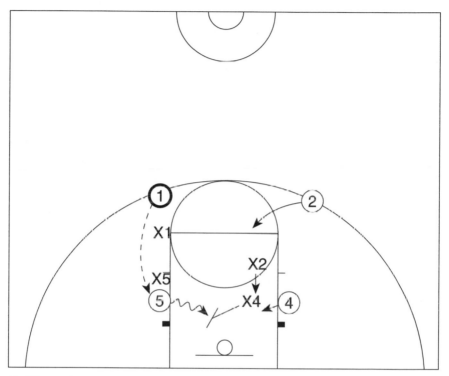

Drill 11   Rotation drill.

12 Double-Down Drill

Objectives

1. To drill low-post moves, shots, and passing.
2. To drill weak-side and strong-side double-down defenses.
3. To drill weak-side attackers on the proper maneuvers to use against double-down defensive tactics.

Procedure

1. 1 and 2 pass ball until pass can go into low post. If the coach intends to post her guards, 1 and 2 pass and screen down.
2. When the pass goes inside to 5, X2 doubles-down on 5. Weak-side double-down is shown in the accompaning diagram; if it had been a strong-side double-down, X1 would have been the double-down defender.
3. X1 can zone between 1 and 2. 5 must either make her move before X2 gets there or find the open guard, 1 or 2.
4. If 5 gets the pass to 2, 4 should try the weak-side pinning maneuver (first presented in diagram 4.1). If 2 gets the ball in to 4 on a weak-side pin, X1 would become the weak-side double-down defender.

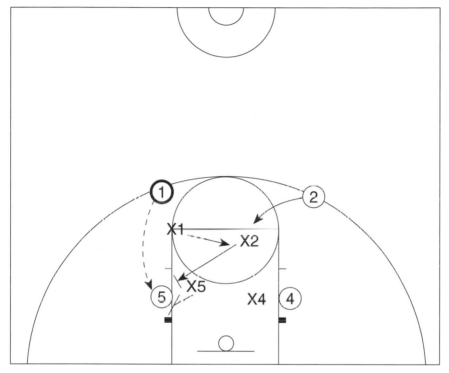

Drill 12   Double-down drill.

13 Complete Low-Post Drill

Objectives

1. To drill on all cuts without the ball.
2. To drill on all inside moves when the ball comes inside.
3. To drill on all defensive stunts on low-post one-on-ones, double-downs, and rotations.
4. To drill fully and completely the savvy necessary to playing the low post, both offensively and defensively.

Procedure

1. Two wing attackers, 3 and 6, are added to the rotation and double-down drills. 3 and 6 do not have defenders, and they may roam from wing to corner. This gives all possible angles for the entry pass into the low post.
2. The diagram shows a flash pivot by 4. X4 cuts 4 off. 1 could pass to 3, who could try to hit 5, the low post. 1 could pass to 2, hoping 2 could dump down a pass to 4. But 1 sees the flash by 4 and X4's proper defense. 1 could try to lob to 4; or if X4 positions himself improperly, 1 could dump down a pass to 4. 1, however, passes to 6 (in the diagram), starting the weak-side pinning maneuver.
3. Once the pass goes inside to the low post, the defense can rotate, double-down, or hedge.
4. All possible low-post attacks are available under this drill format. The coach can even add such team maneuvers as screen away (outside, inside, or both) on all passes to wing players.

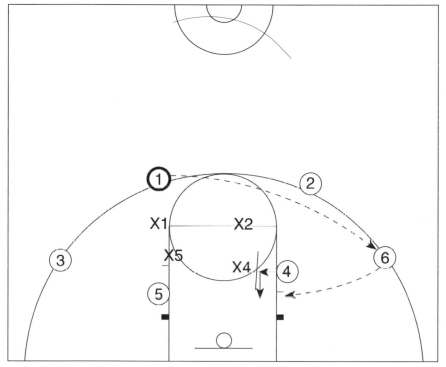

Drill 13 Complete low-post drill.

Becoming a Big-Time Rebounder

Most rebounds carom off into the low-post region, making that area of the court extremely important to winning or losing a ball game. If a coach can develop a post player into an offensive rebounding machine, the team has a leg up on their opponents regardless of the style of play. If a coach has a defensive rebounder or two at the post, he is on his way to developing a great defensive team.

The coach can teach technique to develop rebounders, offensively and defensively, and can also provide rebounding knowledge, some of it based on studies conducted by major universities. It does not do the rebounder any good to be on the right side of the basket when the ball ricochets off the left side. Neither does it do the rebounder any good to be on the side where the ball caroms but standing behind an opponent.

Savvy will place the rebounder where the ball comes off the board. Techniques will put him in front of, or at least to the side of, his opponent. Aggressiveness and determination will allow the rebounder to secure more missed shots. A good offensive rebounder will obtain about one of every five shots he aggressively pursues.

Good low-post rebounders must be able to move their bodies in the air with sufficient skill and timing to be reasonably sure of controlling the ball. They must be able to gain the best possible position both on the floor and on their opponent. They must be prepared to rebound for an entire game.

SAVVY

Coaches, have you ever had a player shoot too much, overpass or dribble to much? We all have. But have you ever had a player rebound too much? Never. All coaches would be happy to secure every rebound.

Savvy begins by anticipating the shot and the likely place the ball will go. The savvy, aggressive rebounder anticipates shots based on his knowledge of his teammates and the team offense. The rebounder can actually begin to move toward the rebound before the shot is released. This aggressive rebounding style allows the offensive rebounder to easily beat the box-out because the box-out has not even begun.

To acquire favorable floor position requires studying a few givens. Wilson Jets ricochet slightly farther than Spalding 100s. Looser rims deaden the ball, causing a shorter rebound. Longer shots carom longer. The smaller the arc, the longer the rebound. Backspin, regardless of the distance of the shot, causes shorter ricochets. Rebounders must compute and negotiate the length of the shot, its arc, the backspin, the ball, and the rim's tightness. Some do it naturally, almost with an innate sense. Others must develop it. But the primary consideration is the area from which the shot is taken.

Shots taken from Area A (diagram 5.1) will rebound into Area A about 95 percent of the time. Shots taken from Area B will carom to Area B over 75 percent of the time. And shots taken from Area C will ricochet to Area C approximately 90 percent of the time.

Shots taken inside ten feet (Area X, diagram 5.2) will rebound back to the shooter about 60 percent of the time. Shots taken from 10 to 15 feet (Area Y, diagram 5.2) rebound away about as often as they come back to the shooter. And shots taken outside 15 feet will ricochet to the opposite side but in the same area (Area A, B, or C in diagram 5.1) about 70 percent of the time.

This knowledge creates a primary and a secondary rebounding area for the retriever. For example, shots taken from the baseline (Area A, diagram 5.1) will rebound on the baseline approximately 95 percent of the time. If the shot is taken inside ten feet (Area X, diagram 5.2), it will rebound back toward the shooter about 60 percent of the time, making the area of the shooter the primary rebounding area and the opposite baseline area the secondary rebounding area. But a shot taken from Area Z on the baseline would produce a primary rebounding area on the opposite baseline and a secondary rebounding area to the shooter's side.

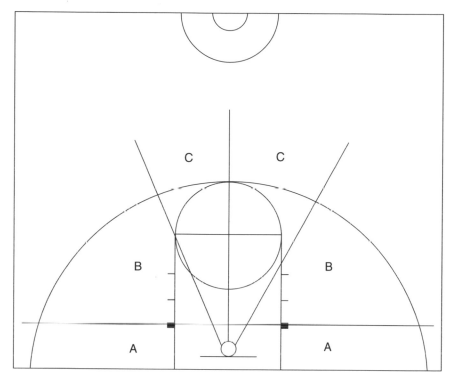

Diagram 5.1

FOUR OFFENSIVE STEPS

An offensive rebounder, armed with the above knowledge, can go to the area where the ball will ricochet. If the offensive rebounder is at least equal to his defender, he has a chance for the second, third, or fourth effort. Being in the area of the carom also enables the offensive rebounder to pick up the fumbled rebound and score the garbage basket.

Positioning

Positioning consists of two parts. First, the offensive rebounder must be beside or in front of his opponent. That requires making the correct move (see next section, "The Moves"). Defenders have the advantage in the low-post area because they have inside position and they have a small area where they must maintain this coverage. Also, the ball comes off the board quickly, giving the offensive rebounder very little time to try to secure a better position. Anticipation and movement are paramount.

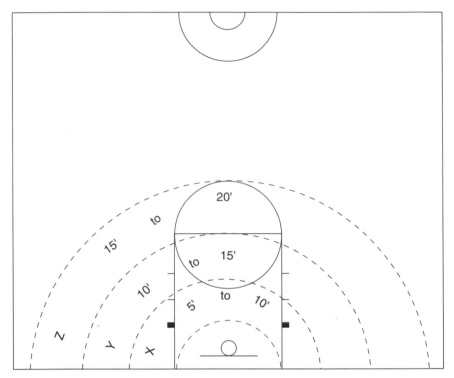

Diagram 5.2

An offensive rebounder must never be satisfied with a position behind a defensive rebounder. If necessary an offensive rebounder must take a less desirable location but be on the side of the defensive rebounder. When it is possible to make a choice, and the offensive rebounder should have one if he anticipates early on the shot, he should use the percentages described in the section on savvy to secure either the primary or secondary rebounding area.

Once the offensive rebounder has established a side or front position, he must maintain it. When the offensive rebounder is behind his opponent and feels that the defender has his weight on his heels, the attacker should step away from the light contact before attempting another move toward the basket. If the offensive player does not lose this contact (once established by the defense), the defender will ride the attacker out of the play.

The Moves

Offensive rebounders can use four moves to obtain proper positioning on their opponents: drop-step roll, spin and roll, jab and go same, and jab and go opposite. Attackers use the drop-step roll only when their backs are to the basket (in a post-up position) when the shot is taken. Attackers use the other three moves when facing the basket. A player needs to learn the drop-step roll and one of the other three, preferably the spin and roll.

Offensive rebounding is a one-on-one battle between the attacker and the defender. It is a game played within the greater game. Usually the winner of the battle of the boards wins the game itself. Rebounders, therefore, must be tireless and relentless in their effort. It is as much mental as physical.

Drop-Step Roll

Low-post players with any offensive skill at all will try to post up their defenders. The defender will either three-quarter or front these low-post attackers. If fronted, the low-post attacker already has inside rebound position. If three-quartered (diagram 5.3), the battle is on.

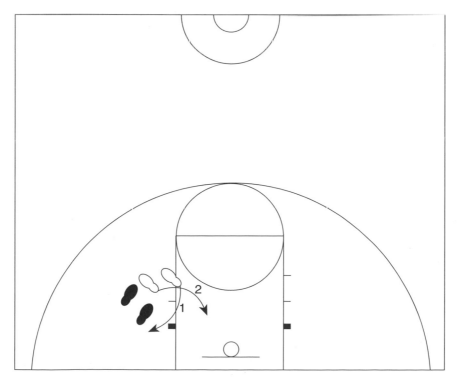

Diagram 5.3

Diagram 5.3 shows the ball in the corner and the offensive low post trying to get position on the defender. If the attacker does get position, the pass comes into the low post and a shot results. If the attacker does not get position and an offensive teammate takes the shot from the corner, the low-post attacker drop-step rolls.

As the teammate shoots, the low-post attacker begins the move for positioning for the rebound. When the shot is taken from the strong side (same side as low post), the low post uses the drop-step roll, unless the defender plays behind her. When the shot is taken from the weak side (opposite side from the low post), the low post uses the spin and roll. The jab and go same or jab and go opposite are auxiliary moves that the low post may use.

When the shot is taken from strong side, the low post usually has her back to the basket. When the shot is taken from the weak side, the low post is usually facing the basket. The high and mid posts are usually facing the basket. Therefore post players need to learn both major moves—the drop-step roll and the spin and roll.

If the low-post attacker on the strong side is being defended by a player behind her, she cannot drop-step roll. This attacker, upon seeing her teammate shoot, turns to face the basket. She now uses the spin and roll (see next section, "Spin and Roll").

The drop-step roll technique has a great advantage—it is simple. It requires at least a three-quartering overplay by the defense before it can be used. Diagram 5.3 shows the overplay by the defense and exhibits the footwork of the drop-step roll. As the low-post attacker sees her teammate shoot (shot must come from the strong side, otherwise the defender would not be in a three-quartering overplay), the low-post attacker drop steps with her right foot. The attacker immediately pulls her left foot even with her right foot. The attacker now has inside rebounding position. She is not, however, in the primary rebounding area; she is in the secondary rebounding area. To hold secondary rebounding position, the low post keeps her defender on her back. To secure the primary rebounding area (see this chapter, "Savvy"), the low-post attacker races across the lane. Regardless of who is there, the low-post attacker has the inside position unless she is blocked out by her defender's teammate underneath the basket. This race across the lane is too often overlooked by the offensive rebounder. Coaches need to stress this move.

Spin and Roll

The low-post attacker uses this technique when she is facing the basket (weak side when the ball is shot, or strong side if the defender is behind the low-post attacker). If the low-post attacker is playing with her back to the basket, she can drop-step roll or she can pivot and face the basket before she begins the spin and roll.

Diagram 5.4 shows the first step of the spin and roll. The attacker crosses her left foot over and places it beside the defender's left foot. The next move is up to the defender. If the defender turns and goes to the basket, the attacker places her right foot beside her left foot and attacks the basket. The attacker is now at least beside the defender.

If the defender pivots to block out or if the defender slides before pivoting to block out (see diagram 5.5), the attacker reverse pivots and now has an equivalent position with the defender. The spin action should take place as early as possible. If the offensive rebounder has anticipated the shot, the spin might occur even before the shot is released.

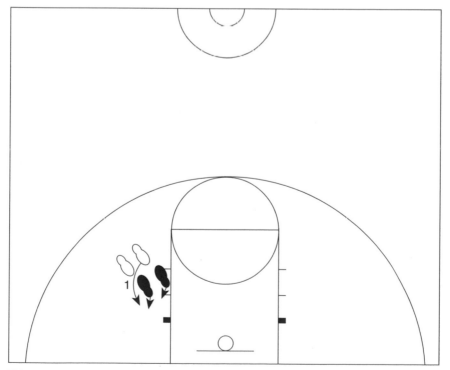

Diagram 5.4

© NBA Photos/Sam Forencich

Figure 5.1   As Moses Malone grabs the rebound in a spread eagle position, he begins a slight turn to the left for the outlet pass.

Low-post offensive rebounders should study the method the defenders intend to use. The three most used defensive techniques are: (1) go to the boards and jump (see figure 5.1), (2) pivot, make contact, and hold the box-out, and (3) slide before pivoting to make contact and box out (see this chapter, "Four Defensive Steps"). If the defense uses the first method, the attacker will be beside her defender on the same side as she began the spin and roll (the right side in diagram 5.4). If the defender uses either of the last two, the attacker, after spinning and rolling, will end up on the left side of her defender (diagram 5.5).

By studying her defender's technique, the offensive rebounder can end up on the side she wishes, not the side the defender prefers. For example, if the defender uses the slide technique, but the low-post attacker wants to end up on the right side of the defender, the attacker would merely begin the first step in the opposite direction (diagram 5.6).

Let's say the ball is shot from the corner. Savvy tells us the primary rebounding area is the baseline (right) side of the defender. By crossing over inside, then spinning and rolling (diagrams 5.6 and 5.7), the attacker is not only on the defender's right side, but also has actually created a larger space for her offensive rebound (the defender is more toward the middle of the court because of the initial move of the attacker).

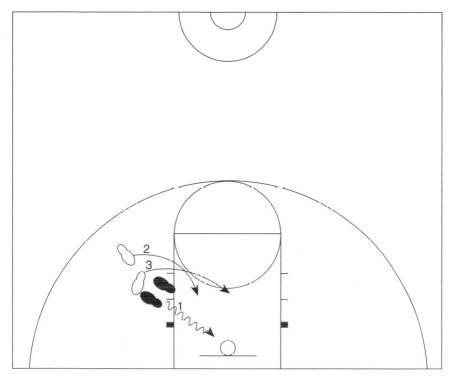

Diagram 5.5

Jab and Go Same

This is a simple method but is usually effective only when the defense does not block out. The attacker steps with her right foot (diagram 5.8) and then brings her left foot beside her right foot. If the defender uses the go and jump technique, the attacker's jab and go same technique is very effective. If the defender slides or boxes out, the attacker jumps all the way around the defender's left side to secure an equal position (and this is hard to do). This jumping around, called jab and go opposite, is shown in diagram 5.9.

Jab and Go Opposite

Diagram 5.9 shows the attacker placing her right foot beside the defender's left foot. As the defender slides, the attacker takes her left foot and places it beside the defender's right foot. Now the attacker must pull her right foot around the defender and place it beside her own left foot. Simultaneously the attacker uses the swim

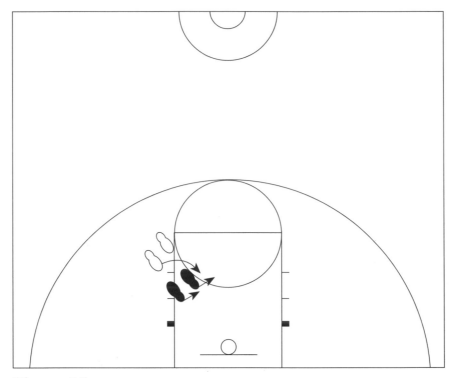

Diagram 5.6

move, putting her right arm on the defender's chest and using a swim stroke. She should not make the swim stroke so strong that she throws the defender off balance. That constitutes a foul.

Both the jab and go same and jab and go opposite are quicker than the spin and roll and drop-step roll. Players should not learn these more advanced moves until they have mastered the spin and roll and drop-step roll. Should a player have difficulty mastering more than two moves, teach only the spin and roll and drop-step roll. A key for offensive rebounding is to stay in constant motion while on offense. This constant motion makes the offensive rebounder's movement quicker, and constant movement makes it far more difficult for defenders to use good block-out technique.

Use drills to learn proper footwork. Using the drills in proper progression insures better learning. Begin by just walking through the drop-step roll. Once the player has learned the drop-step roll, let her walk through the spin and roll. While walking through the spin and roll, the player should learn how the offensive rebounder can choose the side she wishes to end on (the primary rebounding area). Her first step and the defender's method of blocking out determine this.

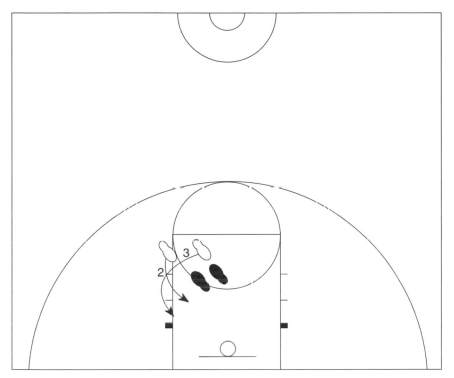

Diagram 5.7

After the player is comfortable with the progress, place a passive defensive rebounder on the attacker. First instruct this defensive rebounder to go down the line of the shot and jump for a rebound. Then the defender uses the slide block-out technique. After the attacker has mastered getting even with the defender on both of these defensive techniques, instruct the defender to use immediate block-outs. After stepping through these three defensive maneuvers, the attacker is ready for live box-outs. The only live block-out drill is one-on-one. The coach shoots from the strong side with the defender three-quartering the low post. The drop-step roll is used. Then the coach shoots from the strong side with the defender playing behind the low post. In this case, the low-post attacker turns to face the defender. This is also how high-post players attack the offensive glass. After facing the defender, the offensive rebounder uses the spin and roll. Now the player moves to the opposite side (weak side) of the lane. The coach shoots and the offensive rebounder uses the spin and roll. During all of this, the coach can pass into the low-post attacker if the defender does not play her correctly.

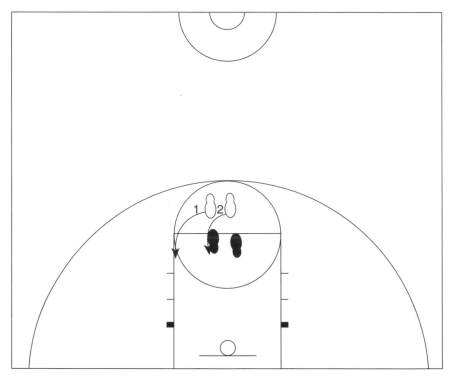

Diagram 5.8

To help develop the offensive rebounder, use the agility tip drill (drill 14). The Superman drill (drill 15) also develops rebounding agility.

I use a multiple-purpose drill (drill 16) to teach offensive rebounding, defensive rebounding, passing, post moves, post defense, and so on. This drill not only teaches the players the basic fundamentals of low-post play, but also teaches them *when* to use each fundamental.

To Grab or to Tip

Players must make a quick decision when rebounding—to grab the ball or to tip it. Most players prefer the tip, but it is not as sound nor as efficient as the grab. If the coach feels a player could have grabbed the ball but tipped instead, she substitutes. This quickly reinforces the grab over the tip.

Encourage players to grab and shoot the return shot while still in the air. If the offensive rebounder can only grab the ball and return to the floor, the player should pump fake to try to get the three-point return shot (see next section, "Grab and Shoot"). If the offen-

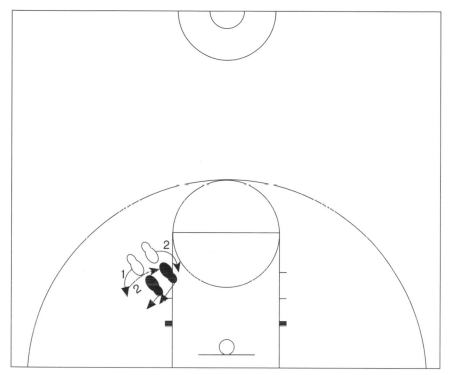

Diagram 5.9

sive rebounder can get only a piece of the ball, the tip is permitted. In other words, the rebounder should keep the ball alive for another offensive rebounder. The preferred order, then, is grab and shoot, grab and return to floor, tip.

Grab and Shoot

The attacker secures the rebound in both hands and quickly places his shooting hand behind the ball. At the same moment, the rebounder-shooter slides his guide hand to the side of the ball. Without returning to the floor, the rebounder shoots the ball back to the basket.

Grab and Return to Floor

Once the rebounder secures the ball with both hands, he tightens his control so that physical contact will not jar the ball loose. If the offensive rebounder cannot immediately shoot the ball back to the basket, he returns to the floor. This is the most common occurrence when rebounding on the offensive end. Now the rebounder pump fakes (no more than twice), trying to get his defender into the air. Once his defender is off balance, the attacker shoots a power layup, hoping for a foul and a three-point play (see this chapter, "Return Shot").

Tip

There are times when bad positioning prevents the offensive rebounder from getting control of the carom. When this happens, the attacker must try to tip the ball. If the offensive rebounder can get enough of the ball to tip it out to a teammate, he does. If only fingertips can reach the ball, the attacker should tip it back onto the backboard, giving one of his teammates a second chance for an offensive rebound.

To teach tipping, use different size balls—a Ping-Pong ball, a tennis ball, a volleyball, a girl's basketball, and a regulation men's ball. Tip ten times right-handed and ten times left-handed (see also rim touching drill; chapter 2). Use all five balls mentioned above. This teaches softness and control.

Rebounding can be made fun by use of the tipping game. Blow up a volleyball to about 15 pounds so it will be extremely active. The coach tosses the ball on the board. Two tippers go up for it. Because of the excessive poundage, the ball will rarely go into the basket and stay; it will likely bounce back out. The first athlete to get a certain number of tips into the basket wins (10 is a good number). This drill is good for leg conditioning and drives your players to make a second, third, and fourth effort (the ball simply will not stay in the basket). It also results in many bumps (physical contact yet keeping control). Instead of a volleyball, you could use a balloon or a softball size Wiffle ball.

Tippers should use one hand so they can reach six inches higher. They need the extra height. The correct tip is a catch momentarily held with fingers, using the thumb to balance the ball, and a tip executed with finger flexion, though a small amount of wrist flexion is acceptable. The arm should have full-elbow extension. Do not bring the elbow down toward the floor. The player must maintain eye contact with the ball at all times.

Return Shot

The return shot is the best possible way to secure a three-point play. Sometimes it is easiest to land and to go back up immediately with the return shot. This occurs when the defender is behind the offensive rebounder. To take this shot, the rebounder explodes back to the basket, throwing his tail back and slightly into his defender. The attacker keeps the ball far out in front of his head. These two maneuvers—contact with the tail to prevent the defender from jumping and keeping the ball in front of the head—prevent the defender from reaching and guarantee that the return shot will not be blocked.

If, after landing, the attacker does not have perfect return-shot position, he should pump fake. To pump fake, the attacker squats as though he intends to explode into the air. Simultaneously he throws his arms into the air, exposing the ball but holding it firmly with both hands. He extends his elbows completely. The fake should look exactly like his shot. If the first pump fake does not get the defender off balance, he should pump fake again.

The shot is preferred to a pass outside, the other option after the second pump fake. Usually a foul will occur if the attacker shoots. The pump fake is taught by use of the power layup drill (drill 17).

FOUR DEFENSIVE STEPS

There are four steps in defensive rebounding: positioning, the moves, the grabs, and the outlet. Each step receives full explanation in sections devoted exclusively to that step.

Positioning

With the exceptions of fronting, three-quartering, or denying the flash pivot, defenders should have inside rebounding positioning. Defenders can maintain this positioning after a shot by sliding the first step with their attackers and then reverse pivoting into a box-out. Defenders may choose not to slide the first step and instead box out immediately. Because of the proximity to the basket, the low-post defender can use either strategy to maintain inside rebounding position. High-post defenders should slide the first step and then box out.

A defender who fronts the low post cannot regain inside positioning against an alert attacker. This position, however, is a secondary rebounding area, not a primary one.

A defender who cuts off the flash pivot (from the weak side) or who three-quarters the low-post attacker has a small battle to wage with his attacker. The defender should begin this battle with a quick reverse pivot on his inside foot. This maneuver should put the defender even with the attacker, a much improved status over his starting position.

The defensive rebounder should catch the ball with vigor; a slap of hands on the ball should be clearly audible. The player should catch the ball with arms fully extended. The defender should retrieve the ball slightly in front of his body rather than directly above it. He should spread-eagle his arms and legs in front of the body and have his tail out. If fast-breaking, a defensive rebounder should turn in the air as he descends to the floor.

The Moves

Defensive rebounding moves are much simpler than offensive moves. The defender already has inside position; he needs only to maintain it. To maintain this advantage, three maneuvers can be taught. To help out on a fronting defender, a fourth maneuver, cross block-outs, can be considered.

Going Down Line of Shot

Immediately when a shot is taken, the defender pivots and goes directly to the board, making himself big by spreading as wide as possible, and getting in a squat position ready to uncoil for the rebound. This was the method used by Coach John Wooden during his tenure at UCLA.

Sliding One Step, Then Boxing Out

Defenders use this method when attackers are quicker and therefore are able to make a fake move before they move to their offensive rebounding positions. By sliding one step with the attacker, the defender does not allow a fake to force him to pivot into a bad position. On the second step, the defender should reverse pivot and make contact. From the low-post position, there is usually not time for a third step. This second step is enough even from the high-post position.

To accomplish a successful block-out, the defender should focus primarily on his man, not the ball or the basket. The defender stays low with a wide body base. He keeps his upper arms parallel to the floor and his lower arms perpendicular to the floor with palms pointing upward. The defensive rebounder should use short, choppy steps as he slides and pivots. The defender's wide body base will permit him to hold his inside position.

Reverse pivots are better than front pivots for inside use. Reverse pivots permit the defender to get a quicker view of the basket, the ball, and the carom. At the high post the defender can use the front pivot to keep his eyes longer on a quicker attacker.

Immediate Box-Outs

This is the best move if the defender is physical. The ball comes off the board quickly at the low post. A strong reverse pivot into an attacker by a physical defender just about guarantees the defender inside rebound position. He needs to maintain it for only a few seconds.

Cross Block-Outs

A defender uses this technique when he has to front a strong rebounder. This is shown in diagram 5.10. When 2 shoots, X5 immediately goes to block out 4 while X4 slides across to block out 5. If 4 is an exceptional rebounder as well, the coach could assign an outside defender to rotate down and block out 4.

High Post

High- or medium-post rebounders have more time before the carom, more space to maneuver. Defensive rebounders must consider this. All the offensive rebounding steps (see this chapter, "Four Offensive Steps") are available to the player crashing the board from the high post. To merely go down the line and rebound places the crashing offensive high post equal to the defender. A wily high-post offensive rebounder would counter the immediate block-out by a fake step before the real move. The defensive rebounder guarding an exceptional high-post offensive rebounder would probably want to slide one step and then block out. This defensive rebounder might even want to front pivot or completely face guard his offensive opponent if the rebounder has the skills of a Moses Malone.

When blocking out at the high post, the defender must consider the three-point shot. It ricochets farther out onto the court, requiring a high block-out. Also, the time of the carom is greater.

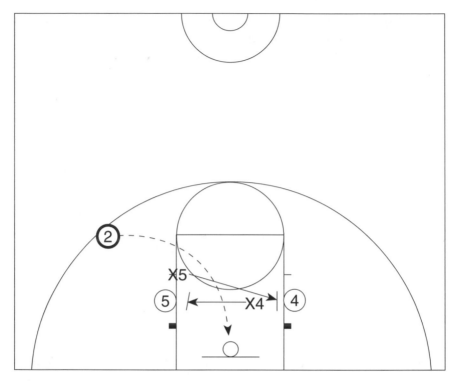

Diagram 5.10

The Grab

Defenders should have inside rebound position. Their attackers should be on their backs. Although this does not always happen, it is desirable. At any rate, defenders should make contact with their assigned attackers.

From this contact position, in which the defender should also be coiled like a spring, the grab begins. The defender throws his tail back into the attacker, bending at the waist, jumping as high as possible as he uncoils. The rebound should be retrieved with both hands touching the ball simultaneously. This should occur in front of the body, over the head, so the attacker would be guilty of an over-the-back foul if he tries for the offensive rebound. The defender should hold the ball firmly with both hands so any contact will not jar it loose (see figure 5.2).

The defender can turn slightly while in the air if the team intends to use the fast break. This will give the defender a step advantage as he converts from defense to offense.

The Outlet

There are two ways to make the pass for a fast break—the outlet pass or the blast-out. Both should be drilled until instinctive.

Outlet Pass

This is sometimes called the ladder pass because it is thrown up the ladder as far as possible. Diagram 5.11 exhibits the ladder on the left side of the court. It is best for the pass to be thrown to the last step if possible (near midcourt). If the defender plays near the half-court line, the pass must be to a shorter step on the ladder, but it should never be shorter than the top of the key.

When the defender, X4 in diagram 5.11 (this is the two-on-two combination drill—drill 16) secures the rebound, he pivots outside, looking down court for a possible fly pattern by a teammate. If the defensive rebounder sees the fly pattern, he should throw the baseball pass. If he sees no fly pattern, he should locate his guard up the ladder and throw a two-handed overhead pass. The break is on.

Blast-Out

If big players can learn to dribble only a few dribbles, this is the best method for beginning the break. X4, in diagram 5.11, first checks deep for the fly as he returns to the floor. If he does not see the fly, X4 pivots on his inside foot, facing the outside boundary line, swings the ball through low, as low as his ankle tops, throws the ball out in front of himself a few feet, and races to bat it to the floor in a dribble. Be careful the rebounder does not catch the throw out with both hands. That's a violation. As the rebounder dribbles his first dribble, the guard on the outside has climbed his ladder, maybe even to the other free throw line extended. When the rebounder sees this guard open, he passes to the guard and goes to fill that lane. The guard takes the ball to the middle to continue the break.

The blast-out usually leaves two or three offensive board players behind, giving the defender-turned-attacker the numbers on the opposite end of the court.

Use drill 18 to teach the blast-out. The drill also helps in pivoting and protecting the ball from tie-ups. Use the combination drill (drill 16) to show *when* (savvy).

The blast-out begins by bringing the ball down as low as possible. The player brings her head and shoulders through as she steps

Figure 5.2   With the rebound securely in hand, Moses Malone looks for the outlet pass.

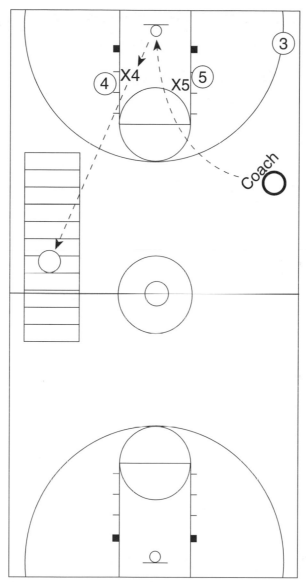

Diagram 5.11

between her two defenders. She brings the ball through last but very quickly. She must toss the ball out before she picks up her pivot foot.

Movement from drill 20 to the two-on-two multiple-purpose drill (drill 16) will teach the players at the low and high post not only the how and the why but also the when of offensive and defensive rebounding.

KEY COACHING POINTS

Proper Body Positioning for Offensive and Defensive Rebounding

Feet

- Space feet shoulder-width apart.
- Feet should be nearly parallel.
- Distribute weight evenly to be able to move quickly in any direction.

Knees

- Flex knees to prepare for the jump.
- Keep body weight on balls of the feet.

Trunk

- Lean slightly forward in direction of the basket to permit movement forward, backward, and sideways.

Hips

- Lower hips to a semicrouched position to give catlike explosive movement toward the missed shot.

Elbows

- Keep elbows out and away from the body to enable the arms to move more freely in all directions and to prevent opponent from leaning into the arms and locking them.

Fingers

- Spread fingers widely apart for better grip on rebound.
- Point fingers up toward the rim.
- Keep hands relaxed, flexible, and dry.

Eyes

- On defense keep eyes on opposing player until box-out is accomplished.
- On offense keep eyes in a wide span using good peripheral vision to locate defenders, to obtain a first indication of a pivot, and to determine direction of rebound.

Body Balance

- Keep weight evenly distributed.
- Be able to move in all directions.

Toes

- Lift heels first. Let weight of body shift down to legs and toes; then push off toes as body leaves floor. A greater spring can be achieved this way.

Jump

- Use high jump principles; do not broad jump. However, jump slightly forward if possible. This prevents an offensive player leaping over the box-out.

Approach

- Extend elbows to their fullest length. Time the jump to touch the ball at the highest point of jump.
- Use two hands and catch the ball; do not slap it.

After Catch

- Bring the ball down in a quick, jerky motion, like plucking an apple from a tree. On the way down begin to spread the feet and legs in a spread-eagle fashion.

After Landing

- Land in a spread, balanced position. A tall player should hold the ball over the head if going for an outlet pass but down very low if planning on a blast-out. A small player should hold the ball very low, nearly to the floor, and begin to dribble away from trouble.

Body Turning

- Turn while in the air after securing the ball to achieve proper body positioning. If rebounding defensively, turn toward the outlet-pass receiver to see the full playing area. If rebounding offensively, turn toward the basket, preparing for the pump fakes or the power layup.

Players have different builds, foot quickness, and size. Many coaches believe in defensive rebounding based on individual skills. A player, in his development, should practice all three defensive techniques, but if one is better for that player, then that is the one to use. The objective is to keep the attacker from the ball; the technique that accomplishes this is the one to use.

SKILLS WRAP-UP

Knowing where to go to get the rebound is crucial. Thus, a section on savvy begins this chapter. Knowing how to get there and what to do when one gets there is of next importance. Hence, sections on offensive rebound and defensive rebounding techniques and methods are presented. Moves are offered for both the offensive and the defensive rebounder. Drills to develop these moves are included.

Adolph Rupp, longtime coach at the University of Kentucky, once stated that the most important fundamental in basketball was passing. If a player can pass the ball, he reasoned, layups will follow. Chapter 6 discusses the importance of passing for all players, including post players.

14 Agility Tip Drill

Objectives

1. To improve jumping ability.
2. To drill going after the second, third, and fourth shot.
3. To increase mobility and agility.
4. To improve the ability to turn in the air while on the way down with the rebound.

Procedure

1. Line up the player facing the basket.
2. The player jumps and touches the rim and on way down she spins 90 degrees, landing with her side to the basket. Upon landing she immediately jumps back up toward the basket, spinning around 180 degrees so her opposite side will be to the basket. The player continues the drill for one-half minute, each time spinning before she lands, each time touching the rim.

 # 15 Superman Drill

Objectives

1. To drill agility.
2. To condition going after the second, third, and fourth shot.
3. To increase mobility.
4. To improve the ability to turn in the air while on the way down with the rebound.

Procedure

1. The player lines up on one big block.
2. The player tosses ball across the board so it will ricochet across the lane.
3. The player takes one step into the lane and power jumps to secure the rebound outside the lane before it hits the floor.
4. The player spins to face the basket while still in air and immediately tosses the ball across the board and races to other side to rebound it.
5. Begin with one-half minute and work up to a minute and a half.

16 Two-on-Two Multiple-Purpose Drill

Objectives

1. To drill rebounding, offensively and defensively.
2. To drill posting, post moves, post shooting, and low post to low post passing.
3. To drill defending the low post.
4. To learn when each of the fundamentals should occur (savvy).

Procedure

1. The coach begins with ball. She may shoot or pass to 3 or 5 or, if X4 is not in good defensive position, to 4.
2. X5 must face the coach so X5 will not know to which side 5 will break.
3. Once 5 is beside X5, live defense occurs. 5 tries to get position and X5 tries to deny this positioning.
4. If the coach shoots, 5 and 4 use offensive rebounding techniques and X4 and X5 use defensive tactics.
5. If the coach passes to 5, 5 uses a quick move to shoot on X5. Now the players begin to use rebounding techniques again. If 5 drop steps to go to the basket, X4 helps to stop the power move (see chapter 4 for offense and chapter 8 for defense). Now 5 can power it up, or 5 can pass to 4 for the shot. In either case the players again use rebounding techniques.
6. If the coach does not shoot or pass to 5, she passes to 3. 3 can shoot (the players use rebounding techniques again, but there will be a different primary and secondary rebounding area) or pass inside to the posting 5. If the ball goes inside to 5, 5 shoots or begins her offensive moves (see chapter 4). If all else fails, 3 passes back to the coach. If 3 passes to 5 and 5 does not have a good move or a good shot, 5 passes back to 3 or back to the coach. Bad shots must be discouraged.
7. When 3 passes back to the coach, 5 can continue to try to get position or can roll across the top of the low-post region to the weak side. This keys X5 to face the coach and 4 to break across the lane. X5 defends 4 and the drill continues. X4 now defends 5.

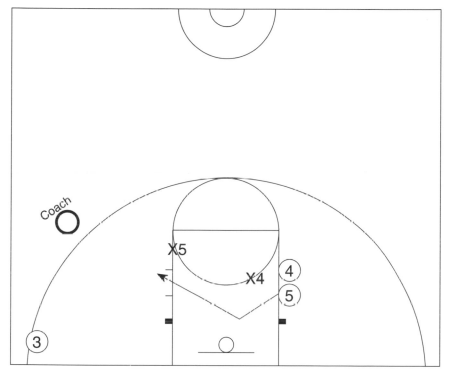

Drill 16 Two-on-two multiple-purpose drill.

17 Power Layup Drill

Objectives

1. To drill drop step.
2. To drill pump fakes.
3. To drill power layup.
4. To condition for continuous offensive rebounding.

Procedures

1. A ball is placed on each big block.
2. 1 steps to a ball, drop steps, pump fakes twice, and shoots a power layup.
3. X1 retrieves the ball, placing it on the just vacated big block. Meanwhile 1 has moved to the other big block. 1 picks up the ball, drop steps, pump fakes twice, and shoots a power layup.
4. The drill continues in this manner for one minute. Then X1 and 1 exchange positions, and the drill goes for another minute. This sequence can be run as long as it is needed.

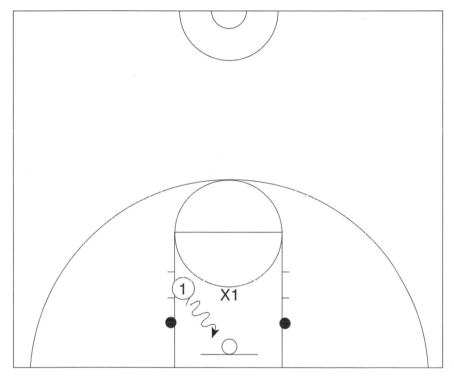

Drill 17   Power layup drill.

18 Two-on-Two Pivoting Drill

Objectives

1. To drill the blast-out.
2. To drill protecting the ball under pressure of two trappers.
3. To drill the step-through move to the guards.
4. To drill trapping.

Procedure

1. Divide squad into groups of three.
2. Two play defense and the middle player has the ball.
3. Allow the defense slight fouling to try to pry the ball loose.
4. The middle player, with the ball, swings the ball through low as she continuously pivots away from one of the defenders. She does this for thirty seconds and then becomes a defender. The defender she replaces becomes the new attacker. In a minute and a half all three would have had a chance to pivot and protect the ball.

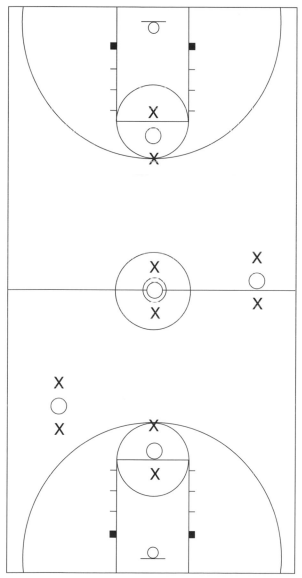

Drill 18   Two-on-two pivoting drill.

19 **One-on-One Block-Outs**

Objectives

1. To drill offensive and defensive rebounding techniques.
2. To drill aggressive offensive and defensive board play.

Procedure

1. Line up two defenders around the foul circle and broken circle. Place two attackers outside the circle.
2. The coach places the ball in the middle.
3. On signal from the coach (whistle, voice, etc.) the defenders try to keep the attackers from touching the ball. Defenders may accomplish this by any of the three defensive techniques described earlier—going down the line of the ball, the slide and box-out, or the immediate box-out.
4. The attackers use their moves to get to the ball.
5. If defenders can hold their block-outs three seconds or longer, they are ready for live competition.

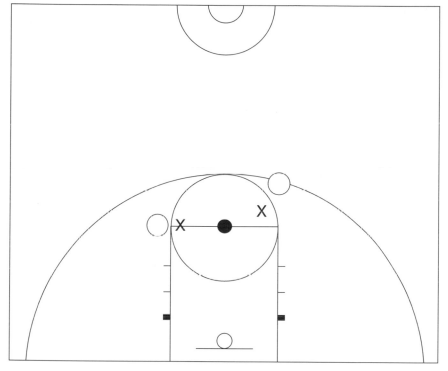

Drill 19   One-on-one block-outs drill.

20 Two-on-Two Rebounding Drill

Objectives

1. To teach offensive and defensive rebounding techniques.
2. To teach aggressive offensive and defensive board play.
3. To teach offensive and defensive moves from the low, mid, and high post.
4. To teach recognition of shot opportunities (if players 1 and 2 cannot get a shot, they pass back out to the coach).

Procedure

1. The next progression is to line up two attackers at the free throw corners. Place a defender on each. The coach dribbles around the circle (or smaller area if she wishes). The coach may pass to 1 or 2 if they are not properly covered. 1 and 2 move up and down the lane line.
2. When the coach passes inside, the receiving player moves to the basket for a shot. The coach, instead of passing, may shoot.
3. When a shot is taken, X1 and X2 block out. 1 and 2 use their offensive techniques to get position.
4. All defenders and attackers must go to the primary or secondary rebounding areas. This requires both offensive and defensive judgment (savvy, moves, and skills).
5. A defensive rebound is followed by an outlet pass or a blast-out. An offensive rebound is followed by a tip, a pump fake and power layup, or a catch and an immediate shot back.

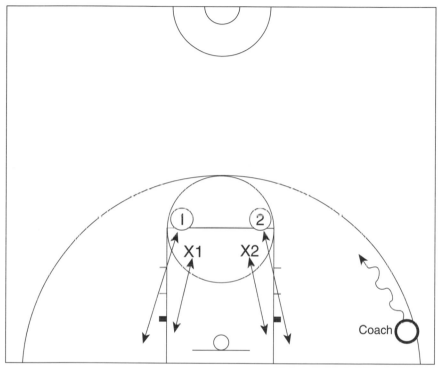

Drill 20   Two-on-two rebounding drill.

6

Becoming a Passer From the Post

Teams work hard to get the ball into the low post. A high-percentage shot results. But defenders react very quickly to stop the low-post player's move for the score, commonly by offering help from the perimeter (double-downs) or from the inside (rotation; see chapter 8, "Rotation and Double-Downs"). When this help happens, the low-post player must be able to stop and pass to an open teammate. Hence the need for high-low, low-low, low-perimeter, and high-perimeter passes.

FOUR STEPS TO PASSING

Before going into passing from high to low, from low to low, from low to perimeter, and from high to perimeter, let's learn the post-passing drill (drill 21 a, b, c, and d). It includes all four possible low- and high-post passes. Should there be defenders, X4 would cover 4, X5 would be on 5, and X6 would cover 6. The 3s, the wings, do not have defenders. It is a continuous drill.

Coaches must decide if they wish to use all possible types of defensive coverage when using this drill, or if they wish to use only their own defensive strategies. The book presents all possible types of coverage, leaving philosophy to the coach.

High-Low

The high-low pass is either a bounce pass or a backdoor lob pass depending on the defensive coverage. Focus on drill 21, diagram b without 4 setting the down screen. You would have the situation illustrated in diagram 6.1.

If defender X5 cuts off 5 by body checking, X5 eliminates the direct bounce pass to 5 but opens the backdoor lob (diagram 6.1). 6 recognizes this. As 5 gives a closed fist signal that he is going backdoor, 6 lobs the ball toward and just outside the opposite rim. 5 springs into the air, catches the ball with both hands, and lays the ball in.

This pass is called a flip lob. The high-post player, 6 (diagram 6.1), raises the ball to the top of his head. With elbows bent slightly, 6 flips the wrist, lobbing the ball just a foot or so over the jumping X5. This pass is delivered with a slight lob, just enough to get by a jumping defender. A higher lob would allow the defense time to recover.

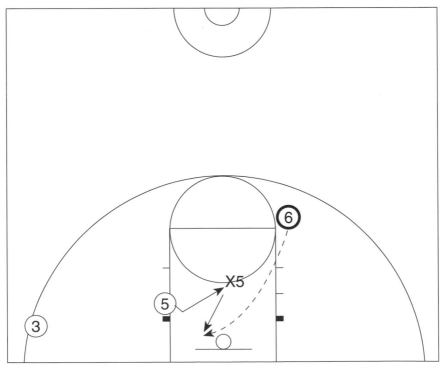

Diagram 6.1

If defender X5 had chosen to play behind 5, and defenders make this mistake often, then 6 can throw the bounce pass into 5. Sometimes this may have to be a step-out bounce pass to get past 6's defender. 6 could throw the direct flip pass to 5. To execute this pass, 6 raises the ball to head level and flips the wrist, passing the ball straight to the receiver. This direct flip must occur after a fake pass; otherwise, X6 will deflect the pass. 5 now makes a move to score. If X5 gets defensive help, 5 must make the pass from low to low or from low to perimeter.

Another option available to 5 and 6 may be reinforced here, although it does not involve low-post passing. That option is a pass from 6 to 3 (high to perimeter) to 5 using the weak-side pinning techniques first described in chapter 4. This pass would be the direct flip pass to the weak-side 3 who, in turn, passes the ball inside to 5.

Low-Low

This option occurs most often when defensive rotation occurs (first seen in drill 11). It is also available in the post-passing drill. In diagram 6.1 suppose X6 overplayed the pass to 6 but missed the pass. 6 drives toward the basket. X5 had to rotate to stop the layup. 5 stepped from the big block toward the basket. Of course, X4 dropped to stop this. 6 must now quickly make the correct pass.

6 keeps both hands on the ball and throws the flip pass toward the backboard side of 5. 5 should have X4 on his back. 5 should receive the pass and shoot the power layup. Alternatively, 6 could reach around X5 to the baseline side and use the bounce pass. The bounce pass should have forward spin to make it travel quicker.

If X4 is late getting to 5—and this frequently happens during a hectic game—6 could execute the quick flip pass. 5 should be moving with both hands high expecting a pass.

If 5 is covered quickly by X4, then the open player is 4. This requires 6 to make the low-perimeter pass.

Low-Perimeter

Low-post passing to the perimeter, in my nomenclature, means two things. The low post passed to the perimeter to avoid congestion (this includes passing to the high post) or to get the jump shot on double-down maneuvers, or the low post passed to a teammate cutting hard toward the basket.

Drill 12 shows the pass under double-down situations (also see chapter 8 for defensive coverage). Because 5 is being double-teamed by X2 and X5, 5 finds 2 open. 2 steps in toward the basket to receive 5's pass for the jump shot. Of course, X1 could have moved over to cover 2, leaving 1 the receiver of 5's pass. 2 could have, in the beginning, cut hard toward the basket. In this case 5 could hit 2 on the cut for the layup.

In the pass to 2 stepping in for the jump shot, 5 needs to execute the quick overhead flip pass. In the pass to the cutting 2, the short bounce pass is preferred. 5 must learn to recognize these situations and 5 must deliver the pass with excellent timing. 5's greatest problem, in the beginning, will be holding onto the ball too long. But with use of the complete low-post drill (drill 13) and the post-passing drill (drill 21) the timing can be corrected. In all double-down situations, 5 would want to pivot to the inside. This makes finding the open teammate easier, and it makes the passing more direct.

Let's use drill 21, diagram c to show how low-perimeter passing can occur in the post-passing drill. Instead of 4 passing to 3 and screening for 6, let's have 4 pass to 5. 4's defender dropped on a double-down defensive maneuver to help 5's defender on 5. 4 can stay outside but step toward the basket for a low-perimeter pass for the jump shot, or 4 could cut hard to the basket for the low-perimeter bounce pass for the layup.

As you can see, the post-passing drill teaches more than just passing. It teaches screening, cutting, posting, post moves, scoring, defense, and rebounding. It reinforces all the techniques of low- and high-post play with a special emphasis on passing. And it uses a minimum number of players so the coach can easily see, evaluate, and correct any mistake.

High-Perimeter

Diagram 6.2 shows a pass from the high post to the strong side wing. 4 can cut to the big block for low-posting maneuvers. 4 can screen away for either the weak-side high post or weak-side low post. 4 could, after screening, roll back to the ball.

Diagram 6.3 shows high-post passing to the weak-side wing. 6 can post, 6 can execute the pinning maneuver, 6 can screen high for 5, or 6 can screen for 4. This pass usually occurs in ball-reversal situations. Most teams reverse the pass against zones and against man defensive teams that really sag from the weak side.

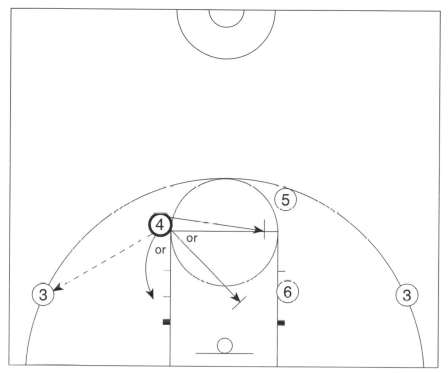

Diagram 6.2

How does 4 make either of these passes? As 4 receives the pass, he should raise the ball overhead with his elbows out. This prevents the ball from being slapped away. 4 overhead flips the pass to either perimeter attacker (see drill 21).

A flash into the high post invites a pass from the perimeter. This high-post attacker, upon receiving the pass, must determine what to do with the ball. He should first consider a give-and-go pass or a give-and-slide maneuver from the perimeter passer. This makes the post player popular. Since he will pass back to an open teammate, the perimeter players will pass more often into the post. The perimeter player knows a pass to the post player is not a pass thrown into a dark hole.

The high post must develop the overhead flip pass—the quickest pass. It is a flip of the wrist without much lob on it. There is just enough lob to get over a jumping defender with arms fully extended.

The high post must develop the sidearm, step-around hook bounce pass to use when he has his back to the basket and a teammate cuts to the basket. He also needs this pass when facing his defender. This is the best pass to a pinning low-post teammate.

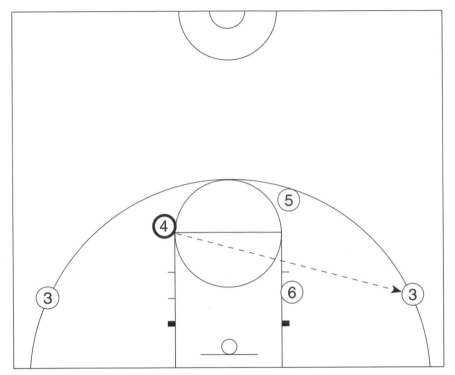

Diagram 6.3

The high post needs the quick reverse pass against zones. This is a quick flip pass, either direct or a semilob.

HOW TO DEVELOP YOUR OWN PASSING DRILLS

Team passing drills should mirror the team's offensive system. It shows creativity on the coach's part and allows his team to learn the movements of the offensive system while drilling on proper passing techniques.

The coach first needs to draw up his offensive play. Diagrams 6.4 and 6.5 show the famed power offense of UCLA during the Wooden era. Many teams still run it.

The coach then takes each part play (each passing option) and creates a drill out of that part play. Out of the UCLA power offense a coach would develop six drills (the proposed drills below follow the passing options numbered in diagrams 6.4 and 6.5)

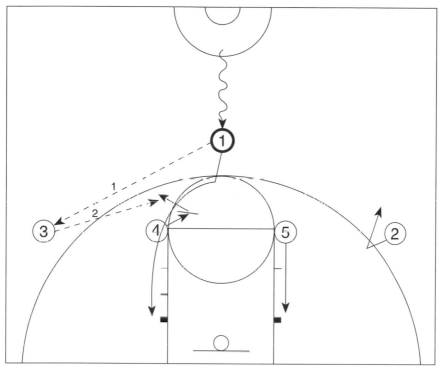

Diagram 6.4

1. A drill for passing to the wing must be created. Defenses will probably overplay this pass. Some may even double-team it. Some will cut 3 baseline and front the inside. There are too many defensive maneuvers for any book to cover, but a coach must consider them all. Each potential coverage might require a different type of pass, so players must first master fundamental passing techniques.

2. The second drill would be a pass back from the wing to the high post. The defense might contest this pass, so the coach should consider a down screen by 4 on 5. These two just exchange positions. The more options a coach considers and drills, the better his team will be at the end of the year. If 3 is double-teamed, the coach might want to consider letting 2 break across the lane, giving 3 three passing options.

3. The third pass would be a pass back to the point guard from the high post, setting up the pass inside to a posting 3, who just screened for 1. This could be considered as one passing drill, although two passes are used.

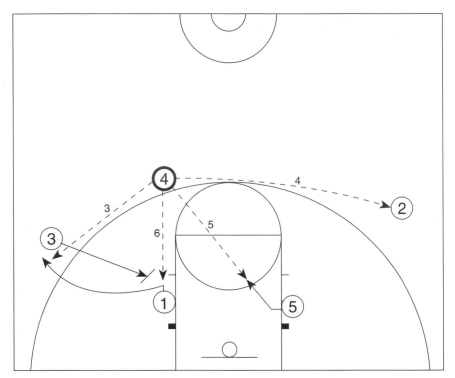

Diagram 6.5

4. A fourth pass would be a weak-side wing pass, setting up the weak-side pinning maneuver between 2 and 5. 2 would have individual maneuvers or can pass inside to the low-post player, 5.

5. 4 could pass inside on the pinning maneuver to 5. Use the passes described in the section on high-low in this drill segment.

6. The last passing drill teaching the UCLA power game is the high-low pass to the point guard.

While learning the UCLA power-game offense, the players also learn to make the bounce pass, the direct flip pass, the overhead flip lob pass, the step-around bounce pass, the footwork techniques discussed first in chapter 2 (should there be a double-team on the initial pass to 3), and so on (figure 6.1). The possibilities are almost infinite. The coach who can recognize all the possibilities and drill on each has an advantage over those who see only some of the possibilities.

Courtesy of UCLA/Norm Schindler

Figure 6.1   The UCLA high-low pass results in a shot.

First, draw your play. Second, study all possible part plays. Third, study all the possible options on each part play. It might be best to combine some of the passing options into one drill. For example, combine options 4 and 5 into a single drill. The better coaches will combine drills as the season goes on.

SKILLS WRAP-UP

This chapter presents all possible passes used by post players. Each passing technique is discussed so the post player will know how to execute each one. A passing drill that includes all possible passes, the post-passing drill, is offered.

Every post option has a section devoted to it—high-low, low-low, low-perimeter, and high-perimeter. Last, a section is presented to help a coach build his own passing drills. Chapter 7 will do the same for screening by discussing all possible types of screens and presenting proper techniques.

21 Post Passing Drill

Objectives

1. To drill good screening and cutting maneuvers.
2. To drill good post-ups, including weak-side pinning, weak-side rolls, and the quick offensive moves off posting.
3. To drill passing from the low and high posts.
4. To drill proper defensive techniques at the low and high posts.

Procedure

1. Put the post candidates at 4, 5, and 6. Use two wing candidates at 3. Put defenders on 4, 5, and 6 but put no defender on either 3.
2. Start with the ball at high post 4. 5 screens down for 6. 6 dips, giving 5 a perfect angle for setting the screen (see chapter 7). 4 can pass to 6, or 4 can high-low pass to 5.
3. If 4 hits 6, 5 can slide back across the lane, using weak-side pinning principles of chapter 4, or 5 can set up his defender, using a dip, for a screen by 4, who rolls across the lane keeping the continuity going (drill diagram 21b).
4. If 4 cannot hit 6, 6 can go backdoor for the lob (drill diagram 21d). 5 can screen across for 6, or 5 can try posting up. If 4 cannot hit 6, 4 can pass to 3 strong side. This keys 4 to screen away (part of your offense) while 5 posts up. If 6 goes for the lob, 5 can screen across the lane for 6. 6 does not assume this; 6 waits for 5. 4 has one other option—to pass crosscourt to 3 on the weak side. 6 could now use the weak-side pinning option (see chapter 4).
5. Anytime a pass comes to the low post, the low-post attacker immediately makes a move to the basket. If this move, say a drop-step baseline, frees the attacker, then another defender must help stop the layup. This means the low-post attacker must make a quick passing decision—low to low, or low to perimeter (to either 3), or to a cutter (4, 5, or 6) coming to the basket. The high-low pass is frequently used to get the ball from the high post to the low post.
6. A high-post attacker can pass high-low at any time—high to the other player coming up from the down screen at the big

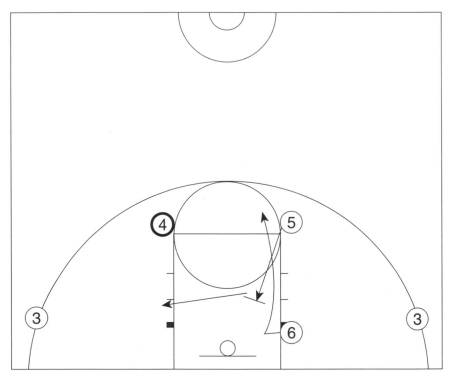

Drill 21a   Post passing drill.

block or high to either wing (strong-side 3 or weak-side 3). When passing to the weak-side wing, the weak-side low post should pin and the high post should screen away. When passing to the strong-side wing, the high post can cut to the low post or screen away.

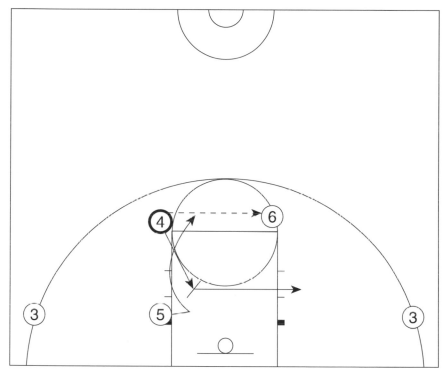

Drill 21b   Post passing drill.

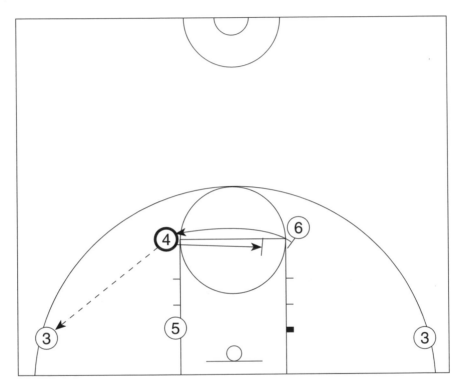

Drill 21c   Post passing drill.

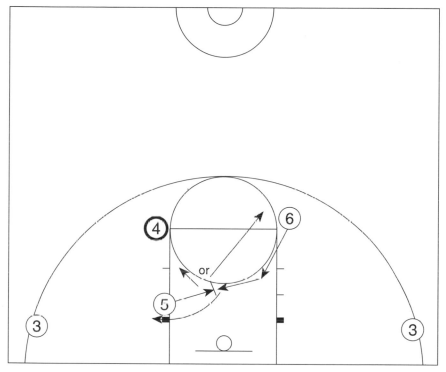

Drill 21d   Post passing drill.

22 High-Low Passing and Pinning Drill

This drill illustrates the techniques of the high-low pass while the low-post attacker is using the sealing move.

Objectives

1. To drill high-low passing skills.
2. To drill sealing, posting, pinning.
3. To drill X4 on defending high-low.
4. To drill 5 to pivot at high post, and in last part of drill, to teach 5 to use high-post fakes.
5. To drill X5 to play high-post defense.

Procedures

1. Line up players as shown. Players rotate from 5 to X4 to 4 to end of line. When X5 is added to the drill, players rotate from 5 to X5 to X4 to 4 to end of line.
2. X4 must defend 4 properly (either three-quartering or fronting) or the coach can pass directly to 4.
3. 5 flashes to the high post. The coach passes to 5, who pivots to face the basket.
4. 4 reverse pivots completely into X4. 4 makes sure his rear makes contact with X4. This contact should occur as the pass is on its way to 5. This contact prevents X4 from regaining position.
5. 5 throws a lead bounce pass to 4, who powers the ball up.
6. If X4 has regained partial position over the top of 4, 5 throws flip lob for power layup.
7. If X4 gained low-side position on 4, 5 throws a bounce pass to the posting 4. 4 uses his moves to score.
8. If X4 gets inside (basket-side) position on 4, 5 passes back to the coach, who dumps a pass inside to the pinning 4. 4 uses his moves to score.
9. As the last part of the drill, put a defender, X5, on 5. In this case, 5 can use his high-post fakes and moves.

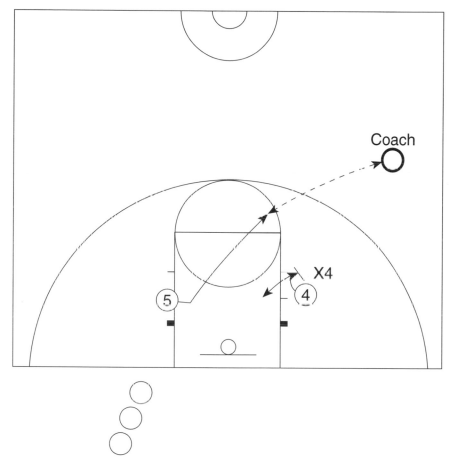

Drill 22 High-low passing and pinning drill.

Becoming a Solid Screener in the Post

Some tall low-post attackers take a long time to develop into scorers. This limits their effectiveness, but it need not limit their ability to help. These slow-developing post candidates can still be used in a pure power method. They can rebound, defend, and screen for teammates. These three basics are more easily and quickly developed. While these tall players are honing their scoring and passing skills, the coach can get game experience for them by teaching the power parts first.

TWO STEPS TO SCREENING

The two steps are reading the screen and setting the screen. By reading and receiving a screen, the post player is getting open for a potential shot by using a screener. By setting the screen, the post player is trying to free a teammate. Sometime during their careers all post players will have need for both. A wise coach will use the less developed, tall low-post player to set screens. The wise coach will also have team methods of setting screens for a good-scoring, tall post player.

Reading Screens

The low post who accepts screens must be able to read screens. This requires a team effort. The coach is a major factor in this. The coach must decide the methods and techniques for accepting (reading) screens.

The accepter of a screen must read his defender. The accepter fakes in the direction of his defender before breaking opposite. Not only does this require his defender to adjust a step or two, it provides the screener with a better angle to set the screen. The accepter then breaks directly off the shoulder of the screener.

Setting Screens

The screener must first know where the ball is. The screener sets the screen so the defensive player cannot move in a direct line toward the ball.

Deceptive fakes by the screener often pay great dividends. The screener can fake going away from the screen, then dip and get the good angle to set the screen.

Screeners must also read the move of the player accepting the screen. This is where teamwork and practice pay off. The screener knows the accepter is going a step or two toward his defender before breaking opposite. This allows the screener to know in advance where he will set the screen. When the screener sets the screen, he must use the half of his body above the line of the ball and the accepter. This makes it more difficult for the accepter's defender to go over the top of the screen. The screener then rolls as the accepter's defender tries to fight under the screen. This compels a switch.

The screener should always look for a quick release for an easy basket. If the screener judges that the quick release is not open, he should roll back to the ball. A quick release means that the player who set the screen does not hold it, but instead, seeing that a defensive mistake is about to occur, races hard to the basket for a pass and a layup. The screen and roll requires the screener to hold the screen, forcing the switch, and then roll back to the ball.

If there has been a defensive switch, the screener becomes the primary receiver because the defender will be behind him. In setting the screen, the screener allowed for this possibility. His screen should begin with a jump stop and a wide base, preparing to receive the blow. The screener does not bring his arms in front of his body. At the exact moment of contact, the screener reverse pivots thus pinning the player leaving the defender on the screener's back.

When there is a switch, the accepter becomes the secondary receiver, and the screener is the primary target. When no switch occurs, the accepter is the primary receiver; the screener is the secondary target. It is important that perimeter passers understand this principle so they will know where to pass the ball.

No new drills are used to teach screening; use the three-on-three passing drill to emphasize screening (see drill 21; chapter 6). The low-low screening action can be used whenever a pass goes from point guard to wing.

This takes care of the down screens and the screens from low post to low post. You may also wish to have your low post screen for a perimeter cutter. Diagram 7.1 illustrates this screen. 2 steps toward his defender, setting him up for the screening angle. 5 reads this move by 2 and sets himself for a perfect angle on X2. This should free 2 for the layup. Meanwhile, 5, after setting the screen, should roll back toward the coach, becoming either the primary or the secondary target, depending on the defense of X2 and X5. Use the same principles to set high-post screens.

If her team is green and is only learning screening, a coach could set up a two-on-two screening activity. The coach could take the ball at a wing and let the strong-side low post screen for the weak side. The coach should be sure that the low post sets the screen correctly and that the accepter reads her defender correctly. The coach could set up breakdown drills of her team offense as screening drills, using the same three steps used for passing. This would teach her offense and at the same time emphasize screening.

TYPES OF SCREENS, STRATEGIES, AND OPTIONS

Regardless of the type of screen being used, the screener would always want to force the defender to go under the screen. Then the screener would roll, keeping this defender on her back. This forces the switch. The screener always wants to be aware of the quick release should a defensive mistake occur. This mistake usually occurs in two forms—both defenders switch to the accepter (in which case the quick release should occur), or both defenders stay with the screener (in which case the screen and roll should occur).

Down Screens

A down screen by a post player for a teammate usually frees the teammate for an uncontested jump shot. A switch leaves the down

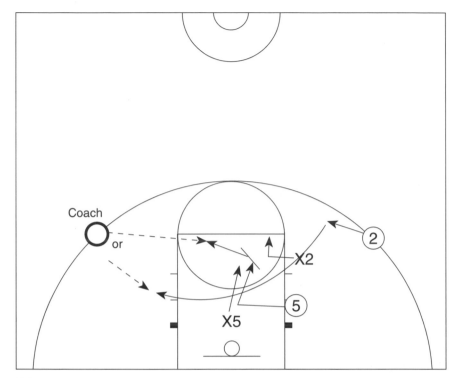

Diagram 7.1

screener with a golden opportunity to seal his teammate's defender near the goal for an easy high-low pass and a power layup.

If the defender on the accepter tries to go over the top, the screener should hold his screen. The teammate should break directly toward the basket for the easy layup.

Back Screen

When a post player sets a back screen, she must give the accepter's defender at least a step to adjust. When back screening for a perimeter teammate at the low-post area, as in the flex offense, the screener might want to set the screen facing the basket. This gives the screener perfect positioning should there be a switch. Without the switch this would give the cutting teammate a layup.

If the back screen is set for a perimeter teammate at the high post, as in the UCLA power offense, the screener's defender usually helps on the cut for a moment. This gives an excellent three-point shooting post player an opportunity to step outside and score the three-point shot.

Up Screen Post to Post

When a low-post player screens up for a high-post player, a switch must occur or a lob pass yields the slam dunk. Following this switch the low-post player should go to the short corner. The high-post player now has the switching defender sealed. In addition the high-post attacker has a large area of the court open for a pass and an easy power move.

Down Screen Post to Post

When a high-post player screens down for a low-post player, an easy jump shot occurs for the low-post accepter unless there is a switch. When this switch occurs, the screener can easily seal the switching defender on his back for the high-low pass and an easy power layup.

Lateral Screens Post to Post

A low-post screener for a low-post accepter is difficult to defend (see chapter 8 for possible defensive maneuvers). A switch, followed by a roll by the screener, gets the ball at high or low post for the high-low game. The absence of a switch usually yields the accepter a layup. The coach can scout teams that use other types of defensive methods and develop a drill to offset any advantage of the defensive method.

Screen by Poor Offensive Post Player

A post player who is not a threat because of poor shooting or poor footwork can still be used as a screener to free the good-shooting players. Indiana University teams coached by Bobby Knight have used this strategy very successfully in their motion offense (figure 7.1). This poor offensive post player will see more hedging and less switching defensive tactics. This is where the quick release would be most advantageous. The poor offensive post player would learn to set screens that defenders could slide over, knowing that his defender would be hedging. At the exact moment of the hedge, the poor offensive post player releases and goes hard to the basket. This will yield some layups, but what is more important is that it forces his defender to hedge less, freeing the poor offensive post player's teammates for easy shots.

Courtesy of Indiana University Athletics

Figure 7.1   Joe Hillman (44) sets a screen for Steve Alford (12).
Notice Steve has rubbed both his defender and the one guarding Joe.

Screen by Good Offensive Post Player

Less hedging can occur against a good-shooting post player. The good-scoring post player would make hedging techniques ineffective. Switching would result in many mismatches. This not only helps the perimeter teammates but also allows the good offensive post player to dominate the inside. Coaches would want the good offensive post player to set many screens.

The Fade

Post players can set screens and fade instead of using the quick release or roll. To accomplish this, the post screener would set the screen, forcing the switch, then fade a few steps in the direction opposite the cutting teammate. This is especially effective for a good-shooting post player.

The fade itself creates a mismatch or allows the post player to shoot the three-pointer. A coach would want to include within the offense ways to allow a good-shooting post player to fade.

Screening for the Screener

A post player steps out and screens for a perimeter cutter while another post player follows the first post player. This second post player screens for the cutter as well as for the first post player. This is difficult to cover defensively.

Another seldom used but successful screen for the screener is to have a post player step out to screen for a perimeter teammate. This perimeter player comes off the screen as if to cut to the basket; but just as the perimeter player clears the screen, the perimeter player stops and sets the screen for the post player.

Many other screening techniques and strategies are available to the creative coach. The coach can develop drills to teach screening as part of the offense by following the same three rules for creating drills for passing (see chapter 6).

SKILLS WRAP-UP

Chapter 7 covers the mechanics, options, and strategies for different types of screens. A wise coach will make use of the poor offensive post player by letting her become a screener until she develops shooting and footwork. But a wise coach will also use the good offensive post player as a screener because it makes her a double threat. She frees not only herself but also her teammates, producing many good shots inside the team's structured offense.

Chapter 8 will show how to defend screens and all the techniques and methods of the first six chapters. This makes the post area a game within the game. It makes the two post players—post attacker and post defender—play a chess game at a high rate of speed and quickness. The victor of this post game is usually the more knowledgeable and more skilled player.

8

Becoming a Tough Post Defender

Low-post defenders see the opponent's entire offense before them. They are in position to make all kinds of defensive decisions to close off offensive attacks. They need to learn not only how, why, and where, but also when. How means the technique; why reveals the reason; where tells the spot; and when denotes the savvy or overall knowledge of the game. All these aspects can be drilled.

SEVEN STEPS TO LOW-POST DEFENSE

There are seven techniques all defensive low-post players (zone or man) need to master: covering the big-block area, denying flash pivots, avoiding the pin, hedging (jamming), defending the high-low, rotating (double-downs), and blocking shots or drawing the charge. These techniques, when executed properly, will make it difficult for opponents to get the inside shot. The sections below will present each of these maneuvers in detail. There will also be a section on defending the high post. Some high-post coverage is included in the section on defending the high-low.

Coverage of the Big-Block Area

The coverage of the big-block area will involve all seven methods discussed in this chapter. This first section, however, will deal primarily with the one-on-one stationary play around the two big blocks. Other sections in this chapter will deal with offensive movement around the big blocks.

As you may recall from chapter 4, the offense prepares itself for three types of low-post defensive play—fronting, playing behind, or three-quartering. When fronted, attackers try to push their defenders out a few feet from the lane, creating a greater area for the lob pass. Defenders, on the other hand, push with their backsides to move the attacker off the big block into the three-second lane. Getting proper floor position becomes a legal shoving match. Once the lob is in the air, the defender leaps back as well as upward, making up any distance between himself and the receiver. The defender stretches his ball-side arm as high into the air as possible. His objective is to deflect the lob pass. If he gets help from a weak-side teammate, the assigned defender may stay to double-team or rotate. Playing in front occurs mostly when the defender fears the offensive moves of the low-post player. The low-post player cannot score if he does not get the ball. Of course this gives the offensive player the inside position for rebounding. Weak-side help is often needed, and the rotation strategy comes into play more often. The coach must decide if the trade-off is wise for his team.

When the big-block defender chooses to play behind his assignment, he concedes the penetrating pass. This means either that the low-post attacker is not an exceptional one-on-one threat or that the one-on-one defender is adept at stopping low-post moves (back-to-basket as well as face-ups). Once the penetrating pass is successful, team techniques—double-downs weak side or strong side, or double-downs by assignment—can be used to discourage one-on-one moves. When the defender plays behind the low post, he must push the attacker out as far from the big block as he can (using body, not arms). Getting proper floor position, again, becomes a legal shoving match.

Defenders should try playing behind attackers who are not exceptional scorers at the low post. Such attackers must first prove themselves before a defender will move to another body position. Playing behind gives the defender the best rebounding position and the best position for blocking shots.

The third and most popular method of individual defensive play is three-quartering (playing on the ball side). The defender keeps his front foot ahead of the attacker's front foot while legally trying to push the attacker away from the ball. All the defender's weight should be on this front foot. By placing the weight on the front foot the defender can quickly step backward, eliminating the back door and the lob. Placing the weight on the front foot allows the defender to pivot to get around the attacker (if the ball is passed to a perimeter teammate of the low-post attacker, see diagram 8.1). This weight placement also permits the defender to pivot for a steal on a bounce or direct pass to the low post or to step back and recover on successful passes into the low post. A quick pivot can also regain defensive rebounding position if a shot is taken from the perimeter (see chapter 5). Three-quartering is a compromise between playing in front or playing behind and combines elements of both strategies.

When using any of the three defensive techniques, the defender wants to force the attacker to a less favorable floor position. The defender does this with proper footwork and legal body contact. The defender must use his body, not his arms, to push the attacker away from the basket and away from the ball. If the ball is high, the defender wants the attacker on the baseline. Conversely, if the ball is low, the defender wants to push the attacker high.

The defender wants to think positioning while he is in transition; he wants to beat his low-post assignment to the big block. Once there, the defender wants to begin the legal shoving match. He wants to gain good floor position while the ball is on its way down court.

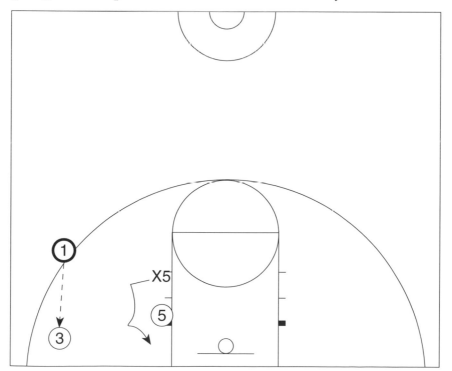

Diagram 8.1

Our first drill involves a simple one-on-one from the low post (first discussed in chapter 4). Use this drill only after players have mastered offensive moves and learned the individual defensive techniques. Diagram 8.1 illustrates the defensive techniques; drill 3 (in chapter 4) displays the execution.

There are two acceptable individual defensive techniques—the two-step (diagram 8.2) or the one-step (diagram 8.3). As 1 passes the ball to 3, 5 tries to post X5 (the defender in diagram 8.2). X5 is trying to prevent this. X5 cannot allow 5 to get his front foot ahead of X5's front foot. If 5 does this, X5 is sealed. X5 cannot go behind 5 without giving up this precious defensive positioning. Should 5 get proper position, X5 must release contact with 5. As X5 releases contact with 5, X5 should place his near arm in front of and on the torso of 5. X5 should use his strength to push against 5's chest. This push should not be so hard that it causes 5 to fall. That is a foul. But this push should be solid enough for X5 to regain position. This is called the swim move—the same swim technique discussed in rebounding (chapter 5).

To accomplish the two-step, X5, in diagram 8.2, moves his left

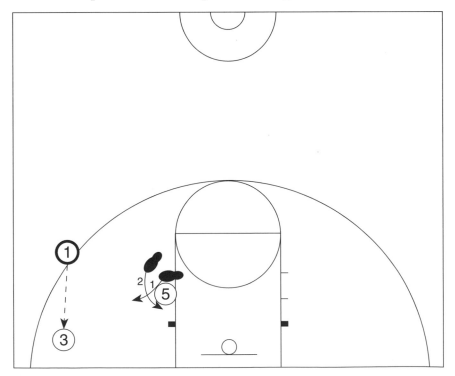

Diagram 8.2

foot to completely front 5. Then X5 moves his right foot to the proper three-quartering position. He makes both these steps as the pass is in the air from 1 to 3 (diagram 8.2). This has the advantage of keeping the three-quartering position. The three-quartering position has just changed from high side to low side as the ball moved from high side to low side. The defender can still prevent the lob, see both his opponent and the ball, keep proper pressure on the attacking pass, and secure the rebound position should 3 or 1 take the shot. The defender is more vulnerable to the drop step should 3 complete the pass to 5 (fig. 8.1).

The one-step (diagram 8.3) is easier to accomplish. All the defender has to do is bring his left foot to a fronting position. The defender does this only from a high three-quartering position, never from a low three-quartering position. When the ball is low, the defender is fronting. The problem with the one-step is that the savvy attacker, 5 in diagram 8.3, will loosen the contact with the fronting defender, X5 (the defender in diagram 8.3). Then, while X5 is trying to find 5, 5 will be reestablishing better positioning (low or high) on

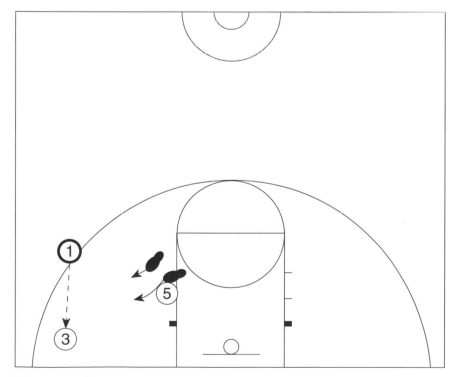

Diagram 8.3

Courtesy of University of Tennessee/Women's Sport Information

Figure 8.1   Carla McGhee (24) has probably just executed a roll and is defended by 10's two-step manuever. If McGhee gets the ball the defender will be vulnerable to McGhee's drop step.

X5. So if X5 intends to one-step, he must step back and feel with both hands for 5. X5 must never let 5 completely loosen the contact. This is a major reason for using drill 11 (chapter 4).

Practice drills 23, 24, 25, and 26 to improve basic defensive moves.

Coverage of the Flash Pivot

A flash pivot into the gut of the low post offers a defensive challenge. When not played correctly, the flash pivot will produce a score and often the three-point play. The flash-pivot cutter can cut directly, or this attacker can use a screen from a teammate.

Regardless of how the flash pivot begins his cut, the defender must deny him the ball. That is, the defender on the flash pivot must play between the ball and the flash pivot.

The defender should know the player he is guarding. If he knows the flash pivot does not shoot the jumper well, for example, the defender can let the attacker get the ball from middle post outward. This would allow the defender to help out in the middle yet still defend his man. See drill 27.

In drill 27, as 5 moves across the lane, X5 has two distinct methods of playing the flash. X5 can open to the ball and slide across (diagram 8.4), or X5 can close to the ball and slide across (diagram 8.5).

To open to the ball, X5 (the defender in diagram 8.4) pivots off his left foot, swinging his right foot to a position parallel to the baseline (diagram 8.4). This leaves 5 unwatched, so X5 must use his hands and body to feel for 5. X5 has a quicker view of the potential lob pass, however, since he is now momentarily watching the passer and not his man.

To close to the ball, X5 (the defender in diagram 8.5) would pivot off his right foot, swinging his left foot to a position parallel to the baseline (diagram 8.5). This leaves X5 facing his assignment. X5 is more vulnerable to the lob, but 5 cannot escape the pressure of X5. X5 does not have to feel for 5; he can see 5. Closing to the ball helps X5 maintain inside position on everything but the lob. Defenders must be quick to use the closing technique successfully.

Avoiding the Pin

Pinning, in my nomenclature, is posting-up from the weak side. Posting-up is a term for gaining position on the strong side (see chapter 4).

Let's use the diagram with drill 27 to explain avoiding the pin. As 1 passes to 2, 5, instead of flashing, moves toward X5 with the purpose of pinning X5 (posting 5 for the pass from 2 back to 1). To pin, as you recall from chapter 4, 5 would want to pivot into X5 as the

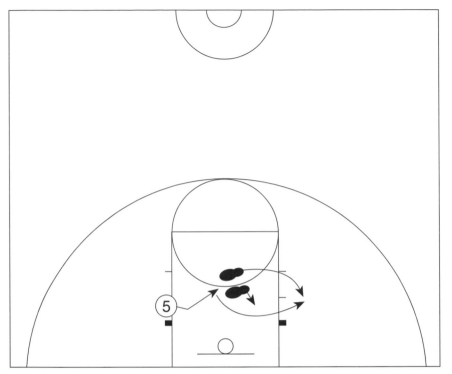

Diagram 8.4

pass comes from 2 to 1. Now 1 can easily pass the ball inside to the posting 5 (who used weak-side pinning techniques) for a quick offensive move.

To avoid the pin, X5 must be aware of its possibility. As X5 sees 2's intention of reversing the ball back to 1, X5 fakes 5 by stepping toward the basket. This requires 5 to alter his route. X5 must avoid 5's body contact. X5 then steps around the high side of 5, preventing the penetrating pass from 1. Should 5 receive the pass successfully, then X5 did not get over the high side. But X5 is in a position between 5 and the basket. X1, the player on 1 if there were one, could double-down (see this chapter, "Rotation and Double-Downs), helping X5 keep 5 from scoring, forcing 5 to pass back to the perimeter.

If 5 should get a good pin and the pass does not immediately come into 5, X5 should loosen the contact from 5. X5 should begin his swim move, putting his inside arm on 5's chest and using his strength to push 5 out of the play. This would compel 5 to try to find X5 before 5 could post X5 again. Meanwhile, X5 has the option of

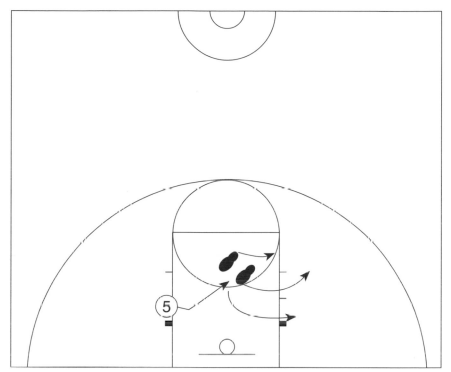

Diagram 8.5

circling either side of 5 and regaining position. X5 should choose the ball side. Again, the perimeter may pass inside while X5 is losing contact; but if X5 does not lose contact, the perimeter has forever to get the ball inside. If the pass does come inside, X5 is still between the attacker and the basket, and the passer's defender can double-down to help force the ball back outside.

Hedging from the Low Post

Hedging means stepping toward a momentarily free attacker and quickly retreating to one's assignment. The low-post position offers the best of all floor positions from which to hedge.

Hedging at the low post requires the defender to keep his hands up. Because the defender is only a step away from his opponent when he hedges, the low-post defender who has his hands up will deflect many passes back to his assignment. By hedging, the low-post defender will cause a momentary pause by the free attacker. That pause gives the free attacker's defender a chance to recover.

Again, there is no switch, no mismatch; switching occurs when the low-post defender calls "rotate."

Along with hedging, the low-post defender can use his position to jam offenses. The low post, like the catcher in baseball, can see everything from his position. If he is a student of basketball, he can constantly jam cutters. This slows down the opponent's attack, throwing the timing off and reducing the efficiency.

To jam a cutter, the low-post defender steps in front of the cutter, making slight body contact. The low-post defender then recovers quickly to his own assignment. The low-post defender can use jamming anytime a post attacker picks his teammate. This slows down the cutter and gives the low-post defender's teammate time to recover to his assignment. Jamming prevents mismatches since the low-post defender does not switch to the cutting guard. Low-post defenders do not call anything. They just jam, or hedge, and get back to their assignments. Their teammates must hurry around any obstacle and recover to their momentarily freed assignment. This jamming or hedging occurs whenever an opponent becomes free near the basket area off screens, off cuts, or off defensive mistakes.

Defending the High-Low

Pressure man-to-man defense has popularized high-low offenses. When the offense gets the ball to the high post, one defender must cover the pass to the low post. There is no weak-side help. Fortunately, there is the three-second lane rule, so the low-post defender has to cover this pass for only three seconds.

Two defensive coverages are available—one by a single player and one that offers help. The low-post defender could front the low-post attacker in the high-low set, but he has no weak-side help against the lob. The high-post defender could help force a bad pass by putting hard pressure on the high-post passer (see this chapter, "Front Foot to Pivot Foot Overplay"). By fronting the low post, only the lob pass is possible. And by pressuring the passer this lob pass could be misdirected, resulting in a turnover. When fronted, the low-post attacker has excellent rebound position. But by pressuring the ball, there is less likelihood a shot will develop. Fronting is effective when the defender is quicker than the attacker.

The other coverage is to play behind the low-post attacker and double-down (see next section, "Rotation and Double-Downs") with the high-post defender when the pass goes inside. The low-post attacker must make his move in a couple of seconds or a three-second lane violation results. And he must make this move under double-teaming pressure. Playing behind is best when the defender is slower than the attacker.

Rotation and Double-Downs

Diagram 8.6 displays the rotation maneuver (see also figure 8.2). It is used here to stop 5's drop-step move, but it can be used to stop a completed lob, to halt a breakaway dribbler, or to stop any open penetrator with the ball. X4 yells "rotate," signaling X2 to rotate down to cover 4. X5 goes toward the area vacated by X4 until he sees X2. Now X5 goes to pick up X2's original assignment.

Instead of just rotating, you can use the rotation to trap. X4, if a trap was called, would double-team with X5. X2 would drop to cover 4, and X3 would have to shade both 2 and 3.

Double-downs can occur from the strong side or the weak side, or you can assign a double-down defender. Rotation is a natural, instinctive defensive maneuver; double-downs are not as natural. Double-downs must be drilled repeatedly.

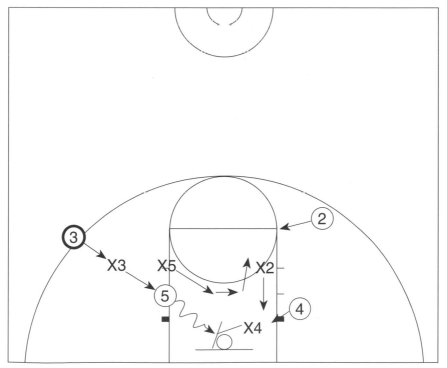

Diagram 8.6

Figure 8.2   Dikembe Mutombo rotates from off the ball to block the shot.

Diagram 8.7 illustrates double-downs. They serve as a trap, so the coach does not need to teach a trap from double-downs as he would when his teams employ rotations. As the pass comes in to 5 from 3, X3 goes to help X5 on 5. This is a strong-side double-down. If X2, instead of X3, had gone to double-down, that would have been

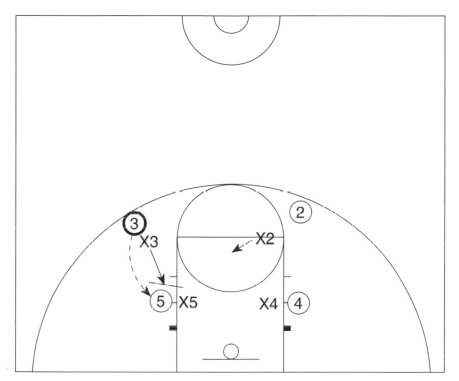

Diagram 8.7

a weak-side double-down. These defenders stay to trap until 5 gives up the ball. When 5 passes out of the trap, the double-down defender, X3 in diagram 8.7, goes back to his assignment. If one of X3's teammates had chosen to cover 3, then X3 would rotate to the open outside attacker. The strength of this double-down is that it leaves X4 inside to cover the weak-side big block, the most vulnerable scoring area. Its weakness is that it leaves a perimeter player open and is not a natural, instinctive defensive maneuver.

Double-downs can also be used with two post defenders. When two post defenders double-down, the defensive team has their tallest players on the double-team and their quickest players shooting the gaps for steals. To execute the double-down with two post players, the weak-side post defender must cheat toward the strong side as the ball is advanced toward the baseline. While this is occurring, the weak-side perimeter player must be cheating toward the weak-side big block.

Rotations have the advantage of allowing defenders to stay matched one-on-one and, like the double-down, prevent the layup.

Rotations usually occur when the defender on the post player fronted or three-quartered the low-post attacker. A rotation is needed to stop the ball. Rotations occur not only when a pass is made inside to a post player who drives to the basket, but also when a perimeter player drives to the basket. The ball scores and it must be stopped.

Double-downs, on the other hand, occur when a pass is made inside to a post player and the defender is playing behind the post player. Even if this post attacker has good foot movement, a double-down would eliminate the next move. But double-downs leave a perimeter attacker open.

If the strong-side passer moves well to open spots and can score, as in diagram 8.7, teams would want to double-down from the weak side. If the weak side cuts well to the basket, teams would want to double-down from the strong side. Coaches must study the strengths of their opposition and decide which double-down strategy to use.

Diagram 8.8 shows a third type of double-down. Let's say the opposition has a weak shooter, or cutter, or passer-penetrator (1 in diagram 8.8). The coach assigns X1 as the double-down defender anytime the ball goes into the low post. If all three perimeter players are effective on offense, coaches can still assign a double-down defender and then rotate the outside three defenders to cover whoever receives the pass from 5. X1 would then have to find the open player.

Another type of team coverage of the big-block area occurs when the defensive team intends to use the double-down as part of their yearlong basic defense. The defender on the low post three-quarters on the ball side as long as the ball stays above the free throw line extended. When the ball is advanced below the free throw line extended, the low-post defender slides behind the low post, pushing the attacker away from the big block with his body. This makes it easier for the offense to pass into the low post, but a double-down defender will arrive as the pass arrives. This double-down defender knows his assignment and cheats toward the post as the ball is being advanced below the free throw line extended.

Once the ball comes into the low post, the defender on the low post cannot allow the baseline drive. This defender must force the attacker to turn toward the doubler (X2 in diagram 8.9). The doubler, X2, must press into the post attacker with his chest, getting as close as possible. If the post attacker tries to step through, a charge will likely be called. Both defenders, X2 and X5 in diagram 8.9, raise their arms as high as possible. This makes it difficult for the low-post attacker to see out of the double-team.

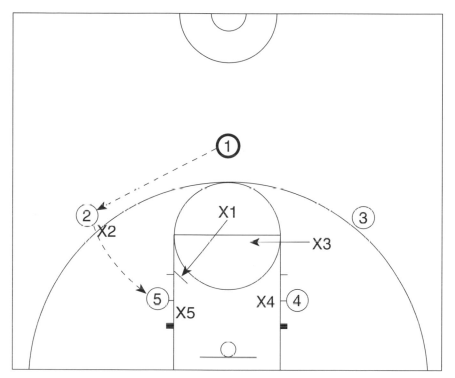

Diagram 8.8

X1 would have two attackers to cover should 5 pass successfully outside (diagram 8.9). X1 reads 5's eyes, gambling at times for interceptions. X1 must use good judgment. More often X1 should arrive at the new pass receiver as the ball arrives. X2, the doubler, rotates to the free player. X1 and X2 must sprint to their new assignments.

This is a good argument to double-down with the opposite post defender when the defense needs to force a turnover. Doubling with the two post defenders puts the tallest two players doubling on the ball. It also frees the three quickest perimeter defenders to gamble for interceptions and to rotate without surrendering a shot if the offense completes a pass out of the double-team.

When considering the teaching of the double-down maneuver as part of the basic team defense, the coach would want to choose one double-down technique, such as the weak-side double-down of diagram 8.9, as her primary double-down tactic. The coach should drill this technique until the double-team is executed properly, until the rotation out of the double-team following a successful pass is habit, and until the outside shot is completely contested. The coach can

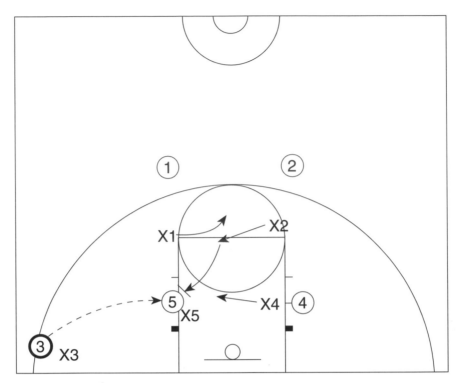

Diagram 8.9

easily teach all other double-downs after the team thoroughly learns any one double-down tactic.

A trap is available in all the double-downs. Coaches would want to rotate the outside two players to cover the three outside attackers. The outside two defenders would play in the gaps of the attackers, studying the eyes of the passer, 5, hoping to steal or deflect any errant pass. If the pass is successful, the double-down defender would have to find the open perimeter attacker.

A fourth type of double-down would have the opposite low-post defender coming over to double-team the powerful post attacker. This puts two big players on the post attacker. The weak-side wing would drop to cover the weak-side low post.

Rotations and double-downs are excellent maneuvers to employ against exceptional post players. Rotations are natural, and they offer a method to stop an otherwise easy score. Rotations can stop an attacker even after the defense has made a mistake. Double-downs can almost shut off exceptional inside low-post players and still allow the team to stay man-to-man.

To Block or Not to Block

This section is presented last by design. It is the coach's most difficult decision. A great shot block artist, and he does not have to be your biggest player, can control the entire low-post area, reducing your opponent's offensive percentages and nullifying much of their offensive strategy. Such a player gives you a great deal more freedom in ways of playing defense. You can offer more pressure without fear of giving the layup; you can extend your defenses; you can trap, even with slower people, without conceding the easy shot. A great shot blocker can carry you to the ultimate championship. Bill Russell was this type of player in the '50s and '60s. Patrick Ewing and Dikembe Mutombo are exceptional in the '90s.

Every year you have players who say they are shot blockers, but few really are. More often than not you will not have a single one. The worst thing for any defense is a would-be shot blocker who consistently leaves his feet to block the shot only to watch a succession of easy layups. A great shot blocker gives your team a tremendous psychological advantage; a weak one will destroy you just as quick.

To block or not to block is your toughest decision. Nothing could be any finer, and nothing, absolutely nothing, could be more harmful.

The other alternative, to draw the charge, is better with most players. Anyone, regardless of size or ability, can learn to draw the charge. The player does not have to possess great skills, only good judgment. And drawing the charge will fire up a team almost as quickly as a blocked shot. In addition, the penalty for the charge is more severe—a turnover, a foul, and a nullified basket (in high schools). That's a triple penalty. It is matched only when the blocked shot results in a fast-break layin and a foul on the other end of the court.

A player must master certain techniques to become an adept shot blocker. Shot blockers must keep the ball in play. They do not want to slap at the ball, knocking it out of bounds; they want to tap it gently to a teammate. Many teams with a good shot blocker, and they are getting more numerous, tip the block to a predetermined area of the court when possible. A teammate is there to secure the tip, and the break is on.

Shot blockers must learn to face the sideline, placing their bodies perpendicular to the backboard. They use the arm nearer the baseline to block the driving shot. They go to the spot near the backboard where they suspect the release (see drill 28). This prevents body contact and the foul. If the shot blocker fails at blocking that particular

© NBA Photos/Thomas Turck

Figure 8.3   The defender blocks the shot with his fingertips and fully extended arm.

shot, he frequently compels a miss. This type of blocked shot occurs most often when the defender has rotated off his opponent and picked up the open driver. The shot blocker, in this situation, must stay on the floor until the driver has left the floor. The shot blocker needs to keep his body between attackers and the opposite big block. This prevents the good passer-penetrator from passing off to a teammate for an uncontested layup.

Opponents who use a double low post for an offensive set give the shot blocker an excellent opportunity to use his ability. The opponent, on the block away from the shot blocker, can get mechanical on his scores, like taking a turnaround jumper rather than penetrating and facing the shot blocker. When this happens, the shot blocker can time his rotation to block the shot easily from the weak side.

Most shots are blocked as a result of a rotation away from the ball. It is far more difficult to block your assigned man's shot without fouling. To block this shot, the defender flexes his knee joints ever so slightly. He has his blocking arm in the air, fully extended (figure 8.3). He waits until his assigned player has obviously left the floor. The shot blocker then leaps quickly into the air, going straight up, trying to tip the bottom of the ball after it has left the shooter's hand. Under no circumstances does the defender allow his wrist to move. The defender should touch the ball only with the fingers, and the arm, hand, and fingers must remain straight in the air. Any downward movement by the arm, hand, or fingers results in a foul, negating good defense.

While playing half-court defense, the coach should designate the spot where the shot blocker will tap the ball. Most often this spot is from the free throw line extended down to the baseline on the side the shot is taken. Shots taken from the front should be tipped to the foul line. A teammate of the shot blocker knows the designated area, leaves his player, retrieves the ball, and begins the break. If a shot blocker is unable to tip to a predetermined area, the defensive teammates still have the advantage of being basket side of the attackers. This basket-side position allows the defenders to retrieve the ball more often than the attackers.

While playing your full-court defense, place the shot blocker near the basket. Now the other four defenders can gamble by setting traps, attempting to steal the dribble, or trying to deflect passes. The opponent will get a few fast breaks, but your shot blocker can handle this. The shot blocker sizes up the opponents as they streak for the basket and makes the smaller attacker or the poorer jumper go for the layup. He forces the taller attacker, usually the poorer passer, to make the final pass. The shot blocker turns toward the sideline at the last moment, using his body to shield the pass back to the opposite big block. He leaves his arms parallel to the floor to deflect any attempted pass to the big block. The shot blocker goes to the spot on the backboard where the smaller of the two players will lay the ball up. It is here he will block the shot.

To use the other option—to draw the charge—a player must use good judgment. The defender's feet must be on the floor before the driver becomes airborne. The defender must take the blow in the torso. He must keep his hands in the air above his body or folded in front of his body to protect himself. The defender must not turn. He may leave the floor, but his jump must be straight up, not out toward the attacker.

Teach the decision to block or to draw the charge using two drills. After players master the how and the why, move to the all-purpose drill (drill 13) to teach the when.

Drill 28 teaches whether to block or to draw the charge. All players participate regardless of size or jumping ability. If a player is not a potential shot blocker, he has only the option of drawing the charge. Drill 29 teaches blocking the shot or drawing the charge.

FOUR STEPS TO HIGH-POST DEFENSE

It is suicide to play high side of the high post. A lob pass to the basket area results in a layup, usually a slam dunk. A defender on the high post, therefore, must play either in a three-quartering position or behind the high post. Under these constraints, the high-post defender must have perimeter help to keep the ball out of the high post.

Know Your Attacker

To defend the high-post attacker, the defender must know the attacker. Is the attacker a good shooter? Does the high-post player drive well? To his right? To his left?

It even pays to know team tendencies. Does the team often use the high-low game? Does the team favor the UCLA power pinning game? The posting game? Or is one-on-one high-post play preferred? Does the team use the high post primarily as a passing position?

High-post attackers have only three individual options—drive to the right, drive to the left, or shoot the jump shot. Three defensive tactics must be mastered to have an effective high-post defense—sag and help on the high-low game, overplay front foot to pivot foot (giving only the drive toward the pivot foot), or pressure and sag (preventing either drive, left or right, but giving up the jump shot under adequate pressure). Consider each of the three tactics.

Sag and Help on High-Low

This defensive tactic eliminates the high-low as an effective offense. The defender on the low post plays behind, and the defender on the high post plays in front of the low post. This defensive strategy, of course, gives the high post the jump shot but eliminates the drives by the high post. It also keeps the ball from the low post.

Front Foot to Pivot Foot Overplay

Use this method against exceptional high-post attackers. A high post who can drive left, drive right, and shoot the jump shot has skills that win ball games.

Something must be taken away from such a high-post player. Playing him straight gives him the advantage. The front foot to pivot foot overplay gives only one option—the drive toward the pivot foot. This drive is the slowest of all moves; and because it is slowest, help from teammates is available.

Diagram 8.10 shows the front foot to pivot foot overplay stance. The left foot is the attacker's pivot foot. The defender places his right foot slightly to the left of this pivot foot and as close to the attacker's body as possible. The defender's wide base places the defender's left foot outside the right foot of the high-post attacker. The closeness eliminates the jump shot. The left defensive foot prevents the attacker from driving toward his right. To do so results in a charge. The attacker must reverse pivot, a very slow move. The defender

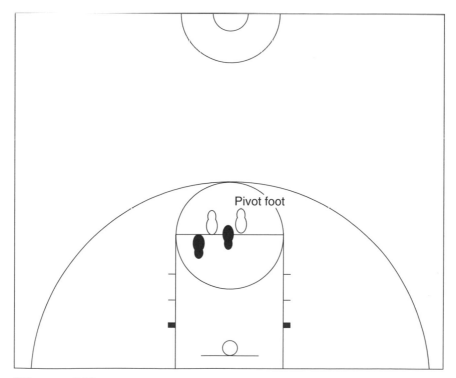

Diagram 8.10

can drop his right foot, readying himself to stop the dribble drive to the defender's right. All the defender's teammates can shade in this direction, even double-teaming if need be. The attacker cannot cross over because of the proximity of the defender's front foot. Usually the high-post attacker passes the ball, the line of least resistance. If the attacker decides to drive, he will usually reverse pivot and drive toward his pivot foot, the slowest of all moves.

Pressure and Sag

The high-post defender drops a step or so, eliminating any thought of a drive. The defender should not use this tactic when the high post is an excellent jump shooter. It should be used when the high-post player drives well but has an ineffective jump shot.

ALL-PURPOSE SAVVY DRILL REVIEW

During all the other drills, both offensive and defensive, presented in the first seven chapters, low- and high-post defensive players constantly make decisions to block the shot or draw the charge, to rotate or double-down, to front or play behind or three-quarter, and so on. That is the purpose of the all-purpose savvy drill presented in chapter 4 (drill 13).

The savvy drill should be restudied here to emphasize the offensive and defensive maneuvers discussed in the first eight chapters. This drill is the culmination of all drills. You now have single-minded drills to improve the fundamentals. You have progressive drills to work on two or three fundamentals together. The savvy drill includes all of these in one drill. If you need to correct one fundamental, go back to that fundamental and use its drill, or use a drill that teaches a few fundamentals and stress the one needed. Then go on to drill 13.

A few of the options of drill 13 are offered in "Key Coaching Points" as a review before moving on to more advanced high- and low-post play.

SKILLS WRAP-UP

The first seven chapters emphasized the attacking point of view, while chapter 8 has covered these ideas from the defensive perspective.

It is all here for the determined athlete who wants to be a great high- or low-post player. It is here for the coach who wants to win. Remember that games are won at the post positions more than any other spot.

The only thing lacking is desire; if I knew how to write desire into a book, I would. But if you have read this far, understanding the all-important details, you have the desire. So if you are a player, pick up that basketball, go outside to the court, and begin to apply what you have just read. If you are a coach, pick up that pencil and begin planning, using the drills and techniques you have just read. See you on the sports pages.

KEY COACHING POINTS

Offensive

1. 1 and 3 try to get ball inside to 5 so 5 can use his moves.
2. 4 can use pinning techniques.
3. 5 can screen for 4. 5 can roll back to the ball or continue to the weak side.
4. 5 can penetrate and pass off to 4 if X4 rotates.
5. 4 can flash to the ball.
6. 5 can work his way out of a double-down (strong side or weak side).
7. 4 and 5 can battle for an offensive rebound should a perimeter player shoot.
8. 4 can receive a pass at the high post and 4 and 5 execute high-low.
9. 5 uses his body to get proper floor and body position.

Defensive

1. X4 plays help-side defense.
2. X5 fronts, plays behind, or three-quarters.
3. X4 denies the flash pivot.
4. X5 gets double-down help from perimeter teammates.
5. X4 rotates.
6. X4 and X5 battle for defensive rebound if a shot is taken.
7. X4 helps X5 defend the lob.
8. X4 and X5 constantly decide whether to block the shot or draw the charge.
9. X4 and X5 recover on passes out from the post.

23 One-on-One, Bull-in-Ring Drill

Objectives

1. To drill 5 to get proper offensive position to receive the pass from the perimeter. Once 5 gets the pass, 5 makes an attacking move. This is also a great offensive drill.
2. To drill X5 how to defend passes inside. The coach can limit the type of passes used. For example, she can eliminate the lob, allow only the bounce pass, and so forth.
3. To drill offensive and defensive rebounding.
4. To drill on leverage and offensive positioning.

Procedure

1. Start by letting 1 bring the ball down from midcourt. This gives 5 and X5 a chance to jockey for proper floor and body position.
2. 1 may pass to 2, 3, 4, or 6. While this pass is in the air, 5 and X5 jockey for position. 1 should read 5's and X5's positions before making her first pass.
3. 1, 2, 3, 4, and 6 may pass inside anytime they wish. They must observe how X5 is playing 5 and pass to the open side. If it is complete, 5 and X5 use the maneuvers in this book to play one-on-one. When a shot is taken, 5 and X5 battle for the rebound.
4. Once the ball is rebounded defensively, it is tossed to the manager. The manager throws the ball to 1. If the ball is rebounded offensively, 5 uses pump fakes to score from the rebound. When the shot is made, originally or off the rebound, players tip the ball to the manager. The manager passes the ball to 1, and the drill continues. While the pass goes from the manager to 1, 5 and X5 jockey for position.
5. The drill can last for two minutes; then exchange 5 and X5. Or you can let the drill continue until X5 stops 5 twice or even twice in a row.

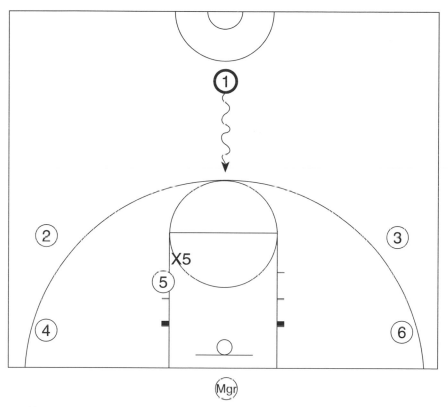

Drill 23   One-on-one bull-in-ring drill.

24 Exaggerated One-on-Two, Bull-in-Ring Drill

Objectives

1. To drill 5's offensive techniques, including low-post passing.
2. To improve X5's defensive tactics.
3. To improve X4's double-down maneuvers (see this chapter, "Rotation and Double-Downs").
4. To drill offensive and defensive rebounding.
5. To drill passing away from the defense to get the ball inside from the perimeter. 5 knows the pass will be made away from the defense, so 5 begins her move in the direction of the pass (see chapter 9, "Post Scoring Theory").

Procedure

1. Same as above except add an X4 to double-team 5.
2. 5 must now move quicker and harder to get open. Once 5 gets open, she must make a quick move to score on two defenders. Or 5 can pass out to an open teammate (they are all open; they may not move).
3. There are two ways the drill can continue now. Whoever 5 passes to can shoot. Now 5, X5, and X4 fight for the rebound and the drill continues. Or X4 can go to cover the pass receiver. Whenever the ball is passed inside, X4 doubles-down (see this chapter, "Rotation and Double-Downs"). 5 can pass out of the double-down or try to score against it.

25 Two-on-One Defensive Drill

Objectives

1. To drill 5 or 7 to move offensively.
2. To improve X5's low-post defensive position on post-ups.
3. To drill 5 and 7 to pin on weak side, post up on strong side.
4. To drill X5 to avoid the pin.
5. To drill offensive and defensive rebounding (chapter 5).

Procedure

1. Penetrating passes can be made only on the strong side. No crosscourt inside passing is allowed.
2. X5 really learns how to avoid the pin (see this chapter, "Avoiding the Pin").
3. X5 must keep 2 and 4 from passing inside to 5 on the left side. But a pass from 2 to 3 would allow 7 to pin X5 as 7 comes across the lane. X5 must learn to avoid this pin.
4. Now 3 and 6 try to get the ball inside to 7. X5 must avoid this posting.
5. If 5 or 7 gets the ball, she makes a quick move to the basket. Or 5 or 7 can pass back outside.
6. After 5 or 7 has touched the ball and passed back outside, the outside players may continue passing or shoot.

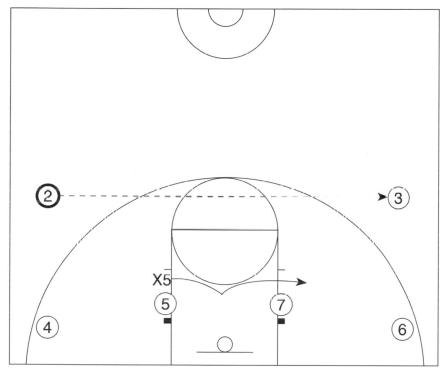

Drill 25   Two-on-one defensive drill.

26 Two-on-Two, Center-Center Drill

Objectives

1. To drill all the offensive maneuvers of low-post to low-post play, including screening and passing.
2. To drill two low-post defenders how to play individual low-post defense, how to help each other out, how to rotate, and how not to switch the low-post to low-post screen.
3. To drill offensive moves, including pinning and posting.
4. To drill the defenders to deny passes to the post and to avoid being pinned (see this chapter, "Rotation and Double-Downs").
5. To drill perimeter passers to study the low-post defender and to pass away from this defender.
6. To drill low-post attackers to make quick moves to the basket.

Procedure

1. Put two low-post players on the big blocks. Put four players on the perimeter as passers without defenders.
2. Begin drill by allowing only passing. This requires X4 and X5 to get to proper strong-side and weak-side positioning.
3. 4 and 5 try to post up but do not move initially. They try to get body position by using the posting and pinning techniques discussed in chapter 4.
4. After the players pass around the perimeter for a few moments, the drill becomes live by permitting penetrating passes. Once 4 or 5 receives the pass, she makes a quick move to score. If defensive help rotates over, the driving center should pass to her teammate on the opposite big block. 4 and 5 can use pinning techniques (see chapter 4) when the ball is opposite them.
5. X4 and X5 must play good post defense (front, behind, or three-quartering). X4 and X5 offer help from the weak side on the lob. They also can use rotation tactics, weak-side or strong-side shot blocking, or drawing the charge, all discussed in this chapter.
6. After the coach is content with strong-side and weak-side defense and offense, she can begin to allow crosscourt move-

ment by 4 and 5. First the coach should allow 4 and 5 to flash to the ball (see section, "Coverage of the Flash Pivot").

7. 4 and 5's next move is to screen for each other (diagram 8.7). They can roll back to the ball after the screen or they can continue to the weak side.

8. There are two ways the defense may choose to play the center-center screen. They can switch or they can use the maneuver exhibited in drill 26b. As the pass goes from 1 to 2, 5 goes to screen for 4. X4 should see the screen coming. X4 always goes over the top of this screen, forcing 4 to go low or not be open. X5 goes the step or two with 5 and steps out to bump 4 (or X5 could merely zone the strong-side, big-block area until X4 recovers). By this time X4 should have recovered on 4, and X5 scampers back onto 5. X4 goes over the top and hurries to the big-block side. This eliminates the switch, which can result in mismatches near the basket. It also requires more concentration and more aggressive defensive play.

9. Offensive players should not force shots. They can always pass the ball back out to a perimeter player.

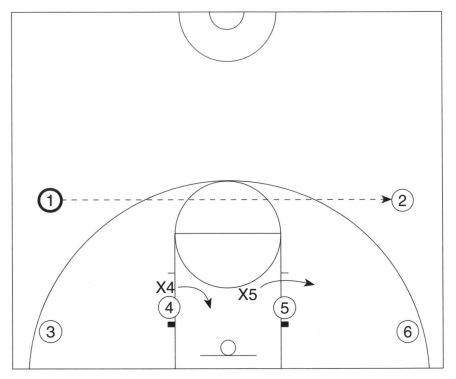

Drill 26a   Two-on-two, center-center drill.

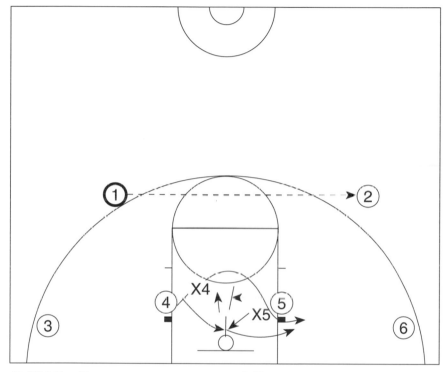

Drill 26b   Two-on-two, center-center drill.

27 Coverage of Flash Pivot Drill

Objectives

1. To drill defending the low-post posting procedure.
2. To drill defending the lob.
3. To drill defending the flash pivot.
4. To drill defending the weak-side pinning maneuver.
5. To drill the attacker on how to pin, how to receive the lob, how to post up the strong side, and how to flash pivot.

Procedure

1. Line up two outside attackers without defenders. Let a low-post attacker (5 in diagram) post up as 1 has the ball.
2. When 1 passes the ball to 2, X5 becomes a weak-side defender. X5, accordingly, sags one step off line with the ball.
3. 5 can now prepare to pin X5, waiting for the pass to come back to 1 (see this chapter, "Avoiding the Pin"). Or 5 can look for the lob pass from 2. But primarily, 5 flashes toward 2 for the pass and an ensuing move.
4. X5 must cut off 5's direct path toward 2 and the ball. 5 moves to the big block on 2's side. 5 tries to post up X5.
5. When 2 passes back to 1, the same options open themselves for the opposite side of court—pinning the weak side, posting the strong side, looking for the lob, and flashing to the ball.
6. If 5 flashes high, X5 cuts him low. If 5 cuts across the lane low, X5 stays on the ball side of 5. X5 must always cut 5 away from the ball. X5 does this by body checking 5 as 5 moves toward the ball. To body check, X5 merely steps in front of 5. If 5 continues, X5 draws the charge. Offensive steps, discussed in chapter 4, will help 5 to get open.

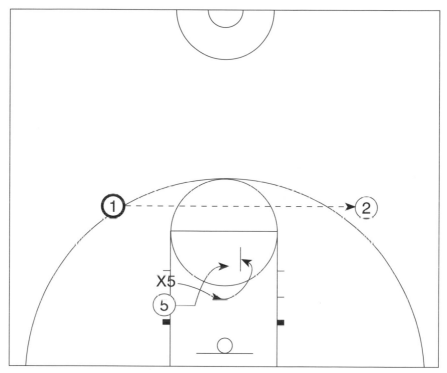

Drill 27   Coverage of flash pivot drill.

28 To Block or to Draw the Charge Drill

Objectives

1. To drill defensive techniques of drawing the charge or blocking the shot.
2. To drill 1 and 2 on two-on-one offensive maneuvers.
3. To drill 2 on offensive power layup techniques.
4. To drill 1 on penetration and dish-off drives.
5. To drill 5 not to take himself out of the play. 5 must recover on 2 if 1 successfully passes to 2.

Procedure

1. 1 rolls the ball to the opposite free throw lane and chases it. He must recover it outside the lane.
2. When 5 sees 1 release the ball, 5 comes over to touch the big block. He then moves up one lane space and touches the small rectangle.
3. As soon as 1 retrieves the ball, he drives toward the basket. 1 can pass to 2 or drive all the way himself.
4. As 1 begins his drive, 2 steps onto the court.
5. 5 moves into the lane or toward the basket to draw the charge or block the shot. 5 must recover onto 2 if 1 passes to 2.

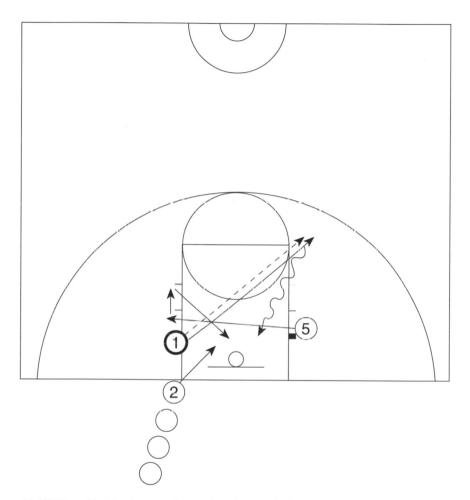

Drill 28a   To block or to draw the charge drill.

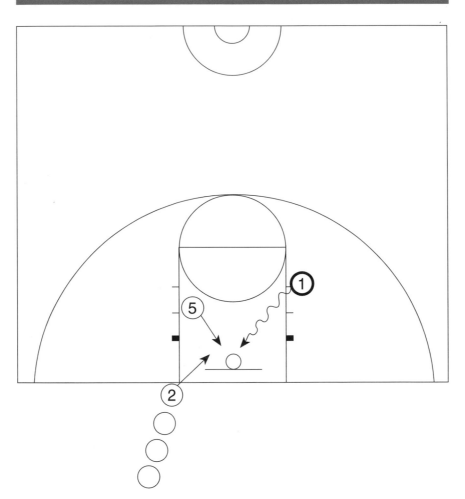

Drill 28b   To block or to draw the charge drill.

29 Quick Shot Blocking Drill

Objectives

1. To drill blocking shots and drawing the charge.
2. To drill offensive power moves or quick jump shots. X5 must turn to find the shooter and then block the shot or draw the charge without fouling.

Procedure

1. The coach tosses the ball into 1, 2, or 3.
2. X5 immediately reacts to block the shot or draw the charge if the offensive player tries the power layup.
3. 1, 2, or 3, upon receiving the pass, uses the power layup techniques or shoots the jump shot.

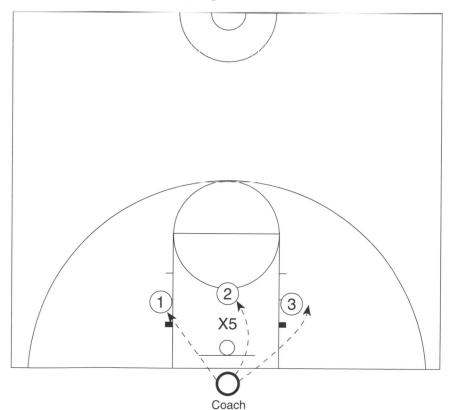

Drill 29   Quick shot blocking drill.

Advanced High- and Low-Post Play

This chapter is for those rare players who have graduated from basic play to advanced play. This chapter is also for those rare teams that have conquered the techniques of the first eight chapters and are truly ready to advance to a higher level of play. Mastering the first eight chapters will allow any team to play at a championship level.

Chapter 9 will give a post scoring theory, five advanced scoring moves from the high and low post that complement the primary and basic moves of chapter 4, three advanced rebounding drills, three new shots which fit in with all the moves presented, an unstoppable high-post screen-and-roll drill, and an advanced passing drill that incorporates all the passing techniques of chapter 6. In other words, this chapter adds to an already complete guide to low- and high-post play.

POST SCORING THEORY

After post players practice moves to a point where they can use them successfully in any ball game, they must develop a well-defined scoring theory. There are many scoring theories. The most basic is to attack the basket by always beginning with a baseline move. Smart defenders quickly figure this out and overplay the baseline side, thereby limiting the effectiveness of the baseline post scoring theory. Next is the power leg theory, which states that the attacker should always pivot on his power leg. Defenders quickly figure this out and just as quickly limit its effectiveness. Both are explained in the next two paragraphs before introducing the direction of the pass theory, which I consider the best option.

Drive Baseline Theory

Some coaches say the best initial move is to drive toward the baseline. There are fewer defenders there they argue. That's true. But, again, to drive baseline always to begin a move before considering another move gives the defense the advantage. The defense will limit its effectiveness. For example, the post's defender would cover the baseline drive from behind the attacker, and while the attacker takes her one dribble baseline to check the defense, a perimeter defender would double-down, eliminating any hopes the attacker has of scoring.

Driving baseline also gives the attacker the poorest shooting angle should the drive be stopped. A defender can force the attacker behind the basket, an unfavorable spot from which to pass. A double-team here would be especially effective.

Turning baseline first also prevents the post driver from knowing where her teammates are. Double-teaming this move, especially if the post driver is behind the board but in the three-second lane, yields many interceptions.

Power Leg Theory

The power leg is the foot opposite the shooting hand; for example, a right-handed shooter's power leg is his left leg. Many post coaches believe their post players should always pivot on their power leg, thereby giving the attacker a more powerful surge toward the basket, more balance for the shot, and more strength to control his defender. In theory that sounds attractive. They argue that the pivot can still occur right or left, depending on the side of the court the attacker is on. They say it is also simpler to teach moves when the attacker always uses the same pivot foot. Also, if a player pivots on his power leg, he will be going in the direction of his greatest offensive efficiency; he will always be shooting using his strong shooting hand whether it is a hook, a jump shot, or a speed shot. The greatest drawback is that the defense will know this and will play to force the attacker toward his weakness (drive toward the pivot foot, drive away from pivot foot, etc.), limiting the effectiveness of this offensive theory.

Attacking in the Direction of the Pass

Attacking in the direction of the pass is the best post scoring theory. When practiced correctly, it is unstoppable.

Coaches using this theory teach their players to pass not to the post player but to pass away from the defender guarding the post. This means there will be three passes coming into the post—the overhead lob pass when the post defender fronts the post, the flip pass when the post defender plays behind the post, and the bounce or direct flip pass when the post defender occupies the three-quarter position.

The explanation of the pass attacking theory begins from the three-quarter guarding position. The post player immediately drop steps and goes toward the goal (one dribble should be sufficient, even from the high post). The post continues toward the basket until he sees the cutoff shoulder of his defender. (The cutoff shoulder could be that of a help defender, such as a defender rotating from the weak side. The cutoff shoulder is the shoulder away from the direction of the drive.) When this happens, it is best to stop, pump fake, and shoot; or stop and pass; or consider another move. Proper defensive positioning would result in a charging foul if the attacker continues. So the post player considers another move—the spin move, taking the attacker far away from his defender, or the half-spin move, getting the defender off balance.

The idea is to attack the basket at all times. The attack in the direction of the pass theory allows this constant movement toward the basket. Again, it begins with the drop step when three-quartered and continues all the way to the basket unless the attacker sees the cutoff shoulder of the defender. The post player then considers another move, one he has practiced many times. If he does not see the defender's cutoff shoulder, the post player continues to the basket. The post player will be fouled, resulting in a possible three-point play.

If the post defender fronts either the high or low post, a lob pass results in a layup. Clear the area behind the post (high or low) and call an automatic lob pass to the fronted attacker. The attacker is going in the direction of the pass. The post player signals this front coverage by showing a fist to the ball handler.

If the post defender plays behind the high or low post, the post player pivots and shoots the turnaround jumper or uses one of his face-up moves (see also chapter 4, "The Move," and this chapter, "Advanced Moves").

To use his face-up moves, the high- or low-post player can shoot the jump shot or pump fake the jumper (or from high post he can use the rocker step). Now he has the direct drive or the crossover drive. The post attacker continues this assault on the basket until he sees the cutoff shoulder of his defender. At that moment, the post (high or low) should stop, pump fake, and shoot; do the spin move; execute the half-spin; or make another move.

Regardless of the defensive positioning, the high-post or low-post attacker has the advantage when using the attack in the direction of the pass theory. The greatest disadvantage, if it can be considered one, is that the post player must learn to move in all directions. He must be able to shoot going left and going right. While in the beginning this might reduce his offensive efficiency, in the end the post will be a complete player. And your team will benefit when championship season approaches. All that remains is for the player to practice, always beginning in the direction of the pass.

ADVANCED MOVES

There are many advanced moves in basketball. Space limitations prevent presenting all of them; it could take forever. I have chosen five because they are usually the first five learned, and they are compatible with the primary two and basic four of chapter 4. I call these the advanced moves.

Up-and-Under Move

Some coaches will argue that this is a basic move. The up-and-under is very compatible to the moves in chapter 4. It occurs at the end of any of the primary two or basic four moves. It is similar to the crossover or step-through. The step-through or crossover is a basic move and occurs at the beginning of a face-up move. The up-and-under occurs at the end of a move, usually preceded by a pump fake. The up-and-under should be the first move learned after the basic four.

When the attacker jump stops at the end of his move, he may find his defender still in perfect position. Without the up-and-under, the attacker's only safe option is to pass to a perimeter teammate. But armed with the up-and-under, the attacker throws his arms upward, fakes with his head and shoulders (a pump fake), and as the defender rises into the air, the attacker assesses his situation. The attacker uses either the crossover or the direct step and ducks under the defender. The attacker, when he steps under, must shoot the ball (or pass it) before his pivot foot touches the ground. If the pivot foot touches the ground, it is a walk.

Usually the up-and-under results in a finesse layup. That is, it is shot from a low position rather than being powered in. To shoot the muscle shot (the power layup), the attacker would need to gather both feet. At the end of a move, this would put the pivot foot back on the floor, and that is a walk.

Of course, the up-and-under can be used as an individual move from the beginning of a move instead of at the end of a move. The post player receives the pass, faces up, pump fakes, and ducks under. Now he has his dribble; he never used it. But he must dribble *before* he picks up his pivot foot. This is the step-through or crossover, a basic move. After using the dribble (and only one should be used—not a slide dribble, but a straight dribble), the player can gather both feet for the muscle shot. Also, after using the dribble and gathering both feet, the player could use another pump fake (should another defender help out, for example), activating all the moves of chapter 4 as well as the dip shot, the hook shot, and the speed shot of this chapter. That is why I teach the up-and-under first.

Step-Back Move

Step-backs are used off the face-up series, off the spins and half-spins, or at the end of any move. Players may step back and then dribble, or they may dribble and then step back. Step-backs are especially effective after the crossover or the direct drive. Patrick Ewing has developed a picture-perfect step-back move.

The mechanics of the step-back are simple, but mastery occurs only after many long hours of practice. It is not as easy as it looks. To execute the step-back, the player merely steps back a step, creating separation from his defender. The jump shot becomes available immediately (see figure 9.1). If the defender rushes at the attacker on the step-back, the attacker can use the up-and-under or any of the moves in chapter 4.

© NBA Photos / Andy Hayt

Figure 9.1   Robinson shoots a step-back jump shot.

A counter to the step-back jump shot is the step-back up-and-under move. The dribble, if kept alive, can even extend the distance a player can move with the up-and-under (step-through) portion of the fake. The step-backs can become as complicated and as advanced as the attacker wishes. It fits coherently into, and can be interchanged at any phase of, the primary two and the basic four of chapter 4.

Let's examine the step-backs from their simplest form to a more complex usage. In its simple form the attacker uses the turnaround move to begin in a face-up position. The attacker immediately

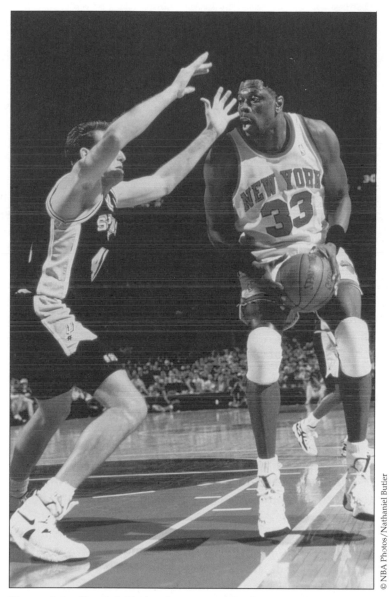

Figure 9.2 Patrick Ewing has one of the best step-back moves in basketball.

steps back with his nonpivot foot as he jumps into the air, creating several feet of separation from his defender, and shoots the jump shot.

If the attacker intends to create greater separation by the dribble, he must begin his dribble before he picks up his pivot foot. This particular phase is extremely hard to master. The player must do extra work to become adept at this phase.

Another phase can occur when the attacker pump fakes and follows the pump fake with an up-and-under move. The attacker, let's say, uses the turnaround and begins his dribble as he steps back. This dribble is to prevent a walk. His defender rushes hard to prevent the jump shot. The attacker pump fakes, making it look like a shot. As the defender leaps into the air to stop the jumper, the attacker, who would have two pivot feet if he ended the dribble with a jump stop, merely steps under the defender for the layup, using either the crossover or the direct step. The attacker can step forward using either foot and not walk if he steps only one and a half steps.

Now let's look at a more complicated multiple move (combination) using the step-back. The attacker drop steps, but since he finds the shoulder of his defender, he spins. At the end of the spin, the attacker steps back, explodes into the air, and releases the jump shot.

There are many other combinations available to the creative attacker from the high and low posts. The player (or the coach) should develop a series or two that complement the physical makeup, experience, and mental development of the young player.

Jump Stop Move

The jump stop move is a very advanced move. When mastered, it is virtually unstoppable. Diagram 9.1 exhibits the jump stop move as a direct drive (or crossover) from the high post. The jump stop move can also be executed from the drop step, the spin, the half-spin, the face-ups, or the up-and-under. The key is to make sure the player is in the air when he picks up the dribble.

Diagram 9.1 shows the high post, 5, driving to his right. 5 sees an obstacle and ends his dribble while leaping sideways into the air, making sure he is in the air before both hands touch the ball. This leap should begin by firmly placing the foot away from the direction of the leap on the floor. Then when the second foot touches the floor, the leap sideways should occur. When 5 lands, it should be on both feet (figure 9.2). Now 5 has the option of jump shooting immediately (usually he is wide open), pump faking then shooting, or pump faking and executing an up-and-under, a spin, or a half-spin. All are available in either direction because 5 has established either foot as a pivot foot. 5, if shooting, has a step and a half in either direction without walking.

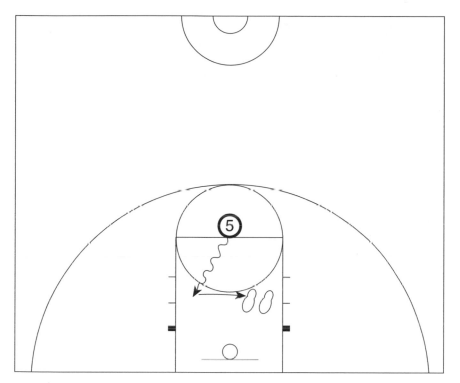

Diagram 9.1

Wedge Move

The wedge move requires teammates to clear out one side of the court for the attacker. (A clear out is not required if the perimeter players are great three-point shooters.) This move can start from farther out than just normal post positions (such as the short corner). The attacker can begin from either the high post or the low post extended.

Upon receiving the pass, the post player waits for his teammates to clear out the side of the court. When a large area has been cleared (usually by cuts), the post front pivots to face his defender. This front pivot has the illusion of keeping the attacker closer to the basket, making the jump shot more of a threat. The post player, as he pivots, places the ball on the hip opposite his pivot foot, keeping both hands on the ball. The elbows are out, and the arms form a wedge formation, protecting the ball (figures 9.3 and 9.4).

From this position, the attacker can jump shoot, pump fake, drive direct, crossover drive, or start his dribble and step-back. Because half of the court has been cleared, the post can take two or three

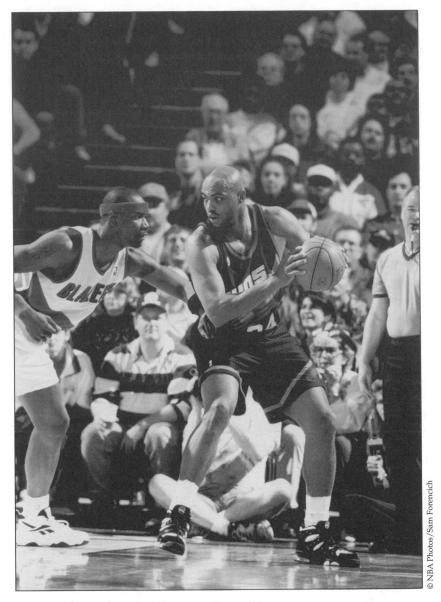

Figure 9.3   Barkley begins the wedge move.

dribbles, setting up one of these optional phases. Should the post begin the wedge move only to find a defender in perfect position, the spin, half-spin, dip shot, speed shot, hook shot, or jump shot is available. If a jump stop is chosen at the end of a dribble, the spin, half-spin, pump fake, up-and-under, step-back, and all other combinations are available.

© NBA Photos/Nathaniel Butler

Figure 9.4 Ewing, in turnaround face-up position, protects the ball from his defenders.

Power Slide Move

The power slide move begins with half of the court being cleared for the attacker (as in the wedge move). The attacker can begin from either the high post or the low post extended. Upon receiving the pass, the post player waits for his teammates to clear out the side of the court. When a large area has been cleared, the post checks over his shoulder at his defender. The attacker begins a slide dribble toward the middle (or baseline) portion of the court. If the defender does not overplay, the attacker continues until he gets in front of the basket. The attacker shoots the dip shot, the speed shot, or the hook layin; or the attacker jump stops and pump fakes, bringing into play the primary two and basic four of chapter 4. If the defender overplays the slide move on any dribble, the attacker immediately drop steps toward the baseline and continues with his power slide move until he shoots the muscle shot (power layup).

If the attacker had begun the power slide toward the baseline, then the opposite sequence of moves would occur. The power slide would continue on the baseline until stopped, then a drop step would put the post in front of the rim. At the front of the rim, the post has available the hook layin, the dip shot, the speed shot, or the jump stop followed by the pump fake and all the moves from chapter 4 and this chapter.

Strength is a prerequisite for the power slide to be most effective. A finesse player could use it, but he would definitely have to reverse his direction when confronted by a defender. A powerful player using the power slide move could overpower the defender and possibly get a three-point play (see figure 9.5). Shaquille O'Neal displays this type of strength in using his power slide move.

ADVANCED SHOTS

Chapter 4 introduced all the shots a great post player would need— the hook layin, the jump shot, and power layup (muscle shot). Here are three more advanced shots. They, like the moves presented earlier, can be placed at the end of any of the moves in chapter 4 or this chapter. All are interchangeable; all are compatible.

Hook Shot

While it is desirable for every post player to have a good hook shot, many modern post players do not. Many coaches do not want their players learning it; they think the shot too hard to perfect. Many think the time spent on this shot does not equal the rewards. So, the hook shot, once considered a basic shot, is now an advanced shot (see figure 9.6).

Figure 9.5   O'Neal executes a power slide to the left.

The hook shot can be used at the end of any move, face-up, or drop step. It is very compatible with the spins, the half-spins, the wedge, the power slide, the up-and-under, and the step-back.

© NBA Photos/Barry Gossage

Figure 9.6   Olajuwon shoots a hook shot.

To properly execute the hook shot, the attacker should have his body perpendicular to the basket. The lead foot should be slightly less than parallel to the basket. The trail foot should leave the ground with a push slightly toward the basket. The shooter should turn slightly toward the basket with his knee that is away from the basket flexed at an almost 90-degree angle. The arm holding the ball should be rigidly straight and extended away from the body. The shooter should bend the arm nearest the basket at about 90 degrees and use it to hold off the defender. As the shooter raises the ball to a high overhead position (at approximately a 150-degree angle with the lower torso), his wrist should flip the ball toward the basket. The flip resembles the flip of the jump shot.

As the shot is on its way to the basket, the shooter should allow his body to continue its turn, landing on the toes facing the basket. Now the shooter is ready for a quick move for an offensive rebound.

The attacker should begin work on his hook shot from close in to the basket, gradually trying to extend the range, much as he would try to extend the range of his jump shot. Not only does the hook shot fit perfectly with all the moves in this book, but the threat of the hook shot forces tighter defensive play, opening up all the moves previously discussed. Tighter defensive play, you may recall, makes the drop step more of a threat.

Dip Shot

After finishing his move, an attacker can find himself facing the front of the basket. Without hesitation, he leaps as high as he can and stretches out his arm until it is nearly to the rim. He lowers his wrist, palm facing upward, and flips the ball slightly over the rim. This is the dip shot (see figure 4.7).

The dip shot must be executed quickly, without a pump fake. The player should use it only when he is near the front of the basket, facing the board, at the end of a move. It is most effective when used with a jump stop (two pivot feet) and with the defender slightly trailing the play.

When this shot is blocked, officials frequently call goaltending, counting the basket. Some advanced players try to use it too far away from the basket. Then, if it is blocked, it is rightly judged a good block.

Speed Shot

The speed shot is neither a hook shot nor a jump shot. It is a slight variation of both.

The shot begins in a sideward position (like the hook shot), but the shooter is turning his body more forward, making the shot also a jump shot. The shooter jumps off both feet, allowing his momentum to carry him toward the basket. He releases the shot on the way up (hence the name speed shot). It is a physical shot, in which contact often results in a foul. As the shooter is turning from a sideward position to one facing the basket, he releases the shot with a slight flip of the wrist. To the unsophisticated, it looks like a throw.

The shooter brings the ball up the side front of the body, where in the hook shot the body protects the ball and in the jump shot the ball is in the shooting pocket. The shooter should be slightly ahead of his defender, landing in a jump stop after a successful move. The shooter should explode quickly into the air toward the basket and his defender, releasing the ball on the way up.

ADVANCED REBOUNDING SKILLS

Rebounding coaches argue whether it is better to have a quick jumper or a power jumper. A quick jumper can be taught to be a power jumper, and a power jumper can become a quick jumper. It is possible, with hard work, to be both. Practice advanced rebounding skills with drills 30, 31, and 32.

ADVANCED SCREENING SKILLS

Many teams are beginning to go back to the old high-post screen and roll, but unless they execute it properly, it will fail. The post player is the key to proper execution. The post player must keep his eye on the ball during the pivot, and his screen must occur on the upper half of the defender covering his teammate. A proper roll will eliminate any chance of a defensive recovery.

Coaches have rediscovered the high-post screen and roll. There is no weak-side help, and a switch on defense puts a smaller guard-type defender on the bigger post-type player.

Diagram 9.2 shows 1, being guarded by X1, dribbling toward the center of the court as 5 sets the screen. 5 sets this screen on the upper half of X1's body, compelling X1 to go behind 5 or allow 1 the driving layup. Of course, X5 could switch, but this would put X5 on an outside shooter and X1 on 5, a much taller post attacker. 1 and 5 can execute the high-low game with almost 100 percent assurance of success.

Once 5 has set the screen on the upper half of X1's body, 5 must observe when X1 decides to step back to get around 5's screen. At this exact moment, 5 rolls. Now 5 has X1 on his back, and X5 must step out to stop 1. Both 1 and 5 have the advantage—1 is probably quicker and more agile than X5, and is probably an excellent outside shooter; and 5 is probably more physical, bigger, and more experienced around the goal than X1. The key remains to execute the roll at the precise moment.

Players should not rush this play. They should read the defensive coverage and attack with penetration. A pass to the roller should occur on a switch, or the dribbler could pull the ball out and pass on the high-low game. If the defenders play it well, the attackers would want to stay under control and simply reset the screen.

ADVANCED PASSING SKILLS

Coaches can develop their team offense while developing their post-passing techniques, killing two birds with one stone. An example of this would involve teaching all the post-passing techniques while running one of your zone offenses.

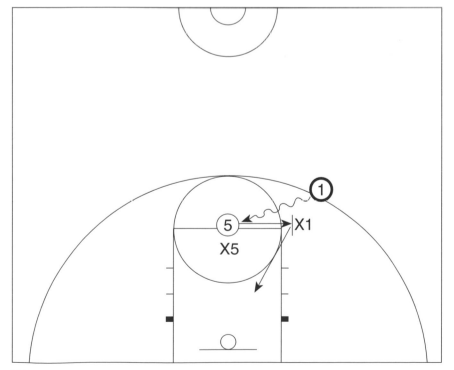

Diagram 9.2

Diagrams 9.3, 9.4, and 9.5 display a zone offense most teams run. As 1 passes to 2, 5 steps to the short corner and 4 flashes to high post (diagram 9.3). 1 and 3 interchange.

If 2 passes to 5, the high post rolls to the low post. 5 can hit 4 on this roll or pass crosscourt to 1 (diagram 9.4). 5's pass to 4 on the roll is emblematic of a pass out of a double-down. 5 would always want to turn away from the double-down to make this pass, turning baseline away from the double-team. 5 could even use this roll by 4 to practice his step-around bounce pass to a backdoor cutter.

Alternatively, 5 could pass crosscourt to 1 (diagram 9.4). This should be an overhead flip pass—a pass often used against a zone defense and one that defensive rebounders should always use as an outlet pass to begin a fast break.

2 could hit 4 at high post (diagram 9.5). 4 should keep this reception high. 4 can practice his step-around bounce pass for the back door to 5. 4 can practice his high-low lob or his direct bounce pass to the posting 5, or he can reverse the ball to 1, keeping the ball high with elbows out.

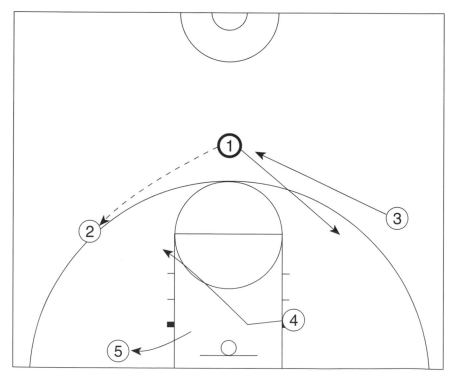

Diagram 9.3

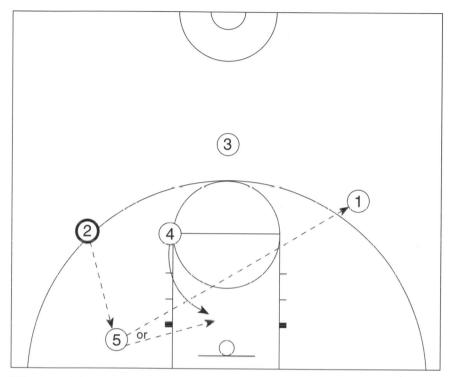

Diagram 9.4

Reversal of the ball by either 5 or 4 passing to 1, or 2 passing to 1, or 2 passing to 3 who passes to 1, signifies the continuity. In the continuity, 4 breaks to the short corner strong side while 5 flashes to high post. Now the offense operates from the right side of the court instead of the left. All the options discussed earlier are again available (5 is the high post instead of 4, and 4 is the short corner instead of 5).

A coach must insist on proper fundamentals while the post players work on their passing skills. The coach can also demand proper execution of the offense from all five players. The best way to teach passing skills is to practice them in the team offense.

SKILLS WRAP-UP

Players have learned five new post moves and three new shots. Chapter 9 also includes three post scoring theories, three rebound-

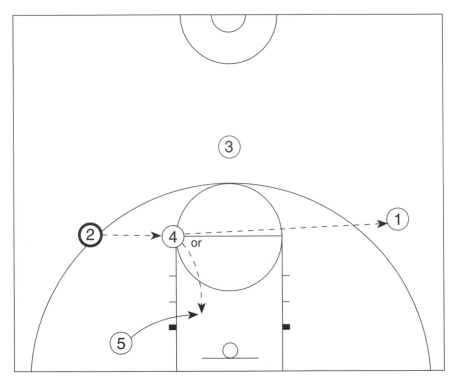

Diagram 9.5

ing drills, a high screen and roll, and an advanced passing drill. A player has everything needed for success around the post area.

IT'S NOW UP TO ATTITUDE

I learned the proper attitude toward post play at a camp I worked when I began coaching. I learned it from, of all people, a ten-year-old nonathlete named Thomas.

At all individual camps some children come to learn the rudiments of the game while others are left by their parents to be baby sat. Thomas was such a kid at this particular camp. He was so pesky he almost drove the camp director wild. He did not want to learn basketball; he wanted to be near the camp director. The camp director was also the head coach, and he wanted to recruit some of the players attending his camp. But he could not get away from Thomas. He called all the workers together and asked for suggestions. He finally got an idea. He had a team picture on a 24-by-36-inch poster hanging on the wall. He had his secretary clip the poster like a jig-saw puzzle into 300 pieces.

The next day when camp started the director handed Thomas the 300 pieces and a few rolls of transparent tape. He gave Thomas another poster and asked him to piece together the one cut into 300 pieces so it would look just like the good poster. Because all the players were dressed alike and all the faces looked so similar, the director knew it would take Thomas several hours to complete the task. He left Thomas in his office with instructions not to bother him until he had pieced the puzzle back together.

The director went into the gym, blew his whistle, and began to give instructions to the other campers. Now he had the opportunity to get to know the players he wanted to recruit. The director had no sooner finished his instructions than the door to the gym opened with a loud sound. It was Thomas yelling proudly at the top of his lungs, "I've done it. I've done it."

The director was startled. "How did you do that so fast, Thomas?"

Thomas flipped the poster over and there was a picture of the director's 6-foot-9 all-American post player. And Thomas replied with the gem I never forgot: "If you put your post player together correctly, your team comes out all right."

 **30** **Power Jumper Drill**

Objectives

1. To condition power rebounding.
2. To drill the power layup (muscle shot) while being fouled.
3. To condition for the second and third effort on rebounding.

Procedure

1. Put a ball on both big blocks.
2. Put two defenders at both big blocks.
3. Send your rebounder to one of the big blocks. The rebounder picks up the ball and explodes up and in toward the basket. (The rebounder can use a pump fake before exploding.) The power rebounder must protect the ball and hold it tightly with both hands. He should lay the shot high on the board to compensate for the foul that is sure to occur.
4. The rebounder goes to the other big block and begins another power layup. The manager secures the made shot and places it back on the beginning big block.
5. This procedure continues until the power rebounder builds his power move and his conditioning.

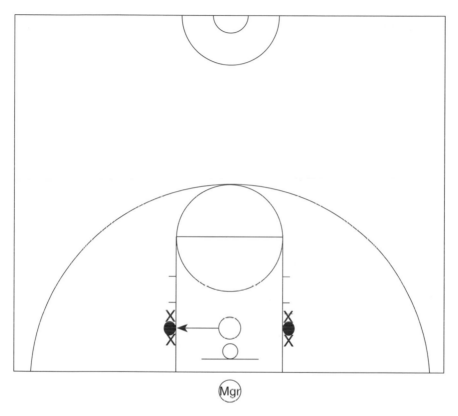

Drill 30   Power jumper drill.

31 Quick Jumper Drill

Objectives

1. To learn quick jumping as an aid to rebounding.
2. To drill a second, third, and fourth effort.
3. To condition for jump after jump after jump.
4. To drill agility.
5. To drill the spin move.

Procedure

1. The rebounder picks up the ball, jumps up toward the rim, places the ball on the rim, and brings it back down as he lands on both feet.
2. The rebounder, immediately upon landing, executes the spin move (with or without the dribble). Now the rebounder is on the other side of the basket. The rebounder explodes upward, touching the rim with the ball. He lands on both feet. He explodes back upward, touching the ball on the rim, and lands on both feet.
3. Upon landing the second time, the rebounder executes the spin move (with or without the dribble). The rebounder is now back on the original side of the basket. The rebounder explodes upward, touching the rim with the ball. He lands on both feet. He explodes upward a second time, touching the rim with the ball, and lands on both feet. He explodes upward a third time. When the rebounder lands, he again executes the spin move. Four quick springs to the basket occur. This can continue until the quick jump is a habit.

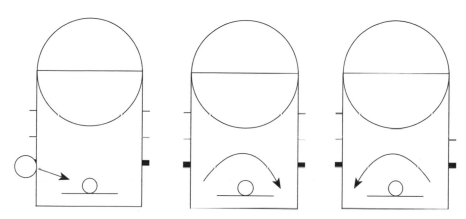

Drill 31   Quick jumper drill.

32 Team Rebounding Drill

Objectives

1. To drill power rebounding.
2. To drill quick rebounding.
3. To drill the muscle or power shot.
4. To drill the hook shot, dip shot, speed shot, etc.
5. To condition second, third, and fourth effort on rebounding.
6. To drill proper positioning for rebounding (savvy).
7. To condition.

Procedure

1. Put three players in the lane around the basket.
2. The coach shoots the ball.
3. The ball remains in play until it bounces more than five feet outside the lane. Players continue even if a basket is scored.
4. If the ball bounces more than five feet outside the lane, the coach begins the drill again, but keeps the score.
5. Scoring five baskets or three consecutive baskets stops the drill. The winner leaves the drill, and the next player in line steps

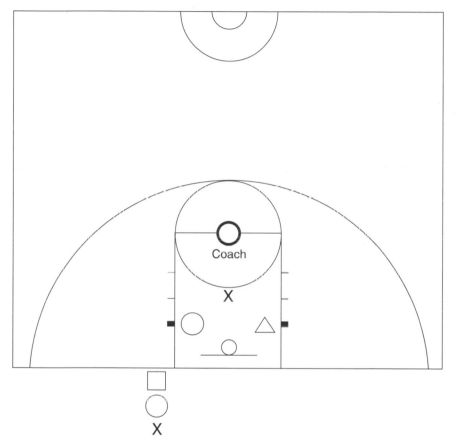

Drill 32   Team rebounding drill.

Index

About the Author

Through more than 30 years of coaching and studying basketball, Burrall Paye has become one of the game's finest teachers. He may be best known for his highly successful, systematic approach for developing post players.

Coach Paye has won more than 61 different basketball championships, had four undefeated regular seasons, and has enjoyed winning seasons for 36 of the 37 years that he has coached. He has won 34 different coach-of-the-year awards, including the 1985 State Coach of the Year (Virginia) and the 1985 National Federation Interscholastic Coaches Association Outstanding Coach. He has been nominated twice for National Coach of the Year.

Coach Paye has spoken at major clinics in the USA, Canada, Mexico, and Europe. He was the featured speaker at the 1987 National Association of Basketball Coaches convention.

His numerous articles have appeared in such magazines as *Scholastic Coach, Basketball Clinic, Coaching Clinic, Pro-Keds Digest*, and *Winning Hoops* as well as in three newspapers. He is the author of eight books on basketball, including the *Encyclopedia of Defensive Basketball Drills, Secrets of Winning Fast Break Basketball, Winning Power of Pressure Defense in Basketball, Coaching the Full Court Man-To-Man Press, Basketball's Zone Presses, Secrets of the Passing-Dribbling Game Offense*, and *Complete Coaching Guide to the Match-Up Zone*.

Paye earned his master's degree in 1965 from the University of Tennessee. He is a member of the National High School Coaches Association and the Virginia High School Coaches Association. He lives in Roanoke with his wife, Nancy, and their son, Patrick. He enjoys golfing, traveling, and playing competitive softball, Wiffle ball, and touch football.

Other Related

Foreword by John Wooden

1992 • Paperback • 240 pp
Item PWOO0446
ISBN 0-88011-446-0
$19.95 ($29.95 Canadian)

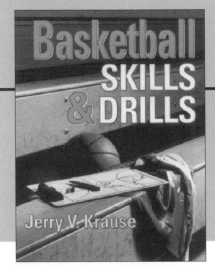

Foreword by Dean Smith

1991 • Paperback • 136 pp
Item PKRA0422
ISBN 0-88011-422-3
$16.95 ($23.95 Canadian)

HUMAN KINETICS
The Premier Publisher for Sports & Fitness
http://www.humankinetics.com/
2335

Books From HK

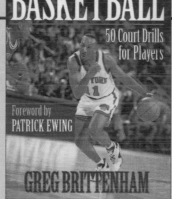

Foreword by Patrick Ewing

1996 • Paperback • 264 pp
Item PBRI0881
ISBN 0-87322-881-2
$15.95 ($23.95 Canadian)

Foreword by Pat Summitt

1995 • Paperback • 264 pp
Item PLIE0610
ISBN 0-87322-610-0
$16.95 ($24.95 Canadian)

Prices subject to change.

To request more information or to place your order,
U.S. customers call **TOLL-FREE 1-800-747-4457**.
Customers outside the U.S. use appropriate telephone
number/address shown in the front of this book.